MW01601738

Small Town Girl, a Memoir

Mount Vernon, WA in the 1940's and '50's

Janet Grimes

CONTENTS

ACKNOWLEDGMENTS

For help in preparing this manuscript I have mainly myself to blame. For advice in selecting a picture for the cover, I have my husband, Bob, to thank. For additional advice and suggestions, thanks to Mary Pennington and Doug Kerr. And for careful proofreading, thanks again to Bob and to Carolyn Simonson.

The section on shopping trips to Seattle was slightly modified from an essay published in the Summer 2009 issue of *Columbia Magazine*.

INTRODUCTION

This is not meant to be a nostalgia piece, comparing my wonderful childhood to the rotten condition of the world today. Occasionally I get email rhapsodizing about the "good old days" when everybody's mother was home all day, children survived without bike helmets and seatbelts, and nobody locked their doors or worried about salmonella despite questionable kitchen habits. Such musings overlook the fact that "stomach flu" was probably mild food poisoning, polio was a regular summer threat, a household canister of DDT was considered an improvement over the fly swatter, and so on.

As a child growing up in Mount Vernon, Washington in the 1940's and '50's, I wished that I had siblings like other children, and that my

parents were young like the parents of children I knew. At our frequent family get-togethers I was surrounded by adults and older cousins, with no one my own age to play with. I wanted my mother to be young and glamorous, to have big breasts and to smoke like my playmate Lonnie Varnadore's mother and her friends. I was ashamed that my father wore overalls to work, whereas other fathers--at least the ones I noticed--wore

1

suits and worked in offices. I wanted many things that money could buy (a new car every few years and vacations to far-away places such as New York, for example). I thought it would be fun to move around the country, living in different states and cities and houses and seeing places I had only heard about.

When I grew up I came to appreciate my good fortune in being born into a family of people who loved me and loved each other. If there were serious disagreements among my relatives, I wasn't aware of them. There were difficult periods, of course, but with them came mutual support. My relatives enjoyed each other's company, which was frequent since most of them lived in the same town or nearby. One exception was

my father's sister, Aunt Carol, and her family, who lived across the state in Spokane. But they came to Mount Vernon regularly to visit for lengthy periods, staying almost next door with Grandpa and later Aunt Ruth. Other exceptions were various cousins of my parents, who made occasional visits. I will forever be grateful for the sense of security, of belonging, of roots that this provided.

Photographs reinforced this connection. In Grandma's writing desk was a drawer filled with old pictures. Some were mounted on heavy cardboard, embossed with scrolled designs and stamped with the photographer's name and location. Others were in folders that opened

back upon themselves to form a little stand. Most were formal portraits of individuals or couples or families, posed in studios with distinctive backdrops; but some were informal groupings, and occasionally there was an action shot crudely mounted on cardboard by an amateur.

2

There even were a couple of tintypes.

When I stayed overnight with Grandma she told stories of her own childhood, her Mama and Papa, her big brother and four older sisters-- some of whom I knew, now old like Grandma. The pictures in her writing desk gave faces to the names in her bedtime tales. "Who is this, Grandma?" I would ask, pointing to an old couple in an oval portrait.

"That's Mama and Papa; they're gone now."

"And this?"

"That's Lennie and me when we first were married." Lennie was Grandpa Ward. He had been dead a long time.

"Who are these kids?"

"Those are Margaret and Buster, Walter's children."

"Who's Walter?"

As this ritual was repeated over the years, gradually I acquired a sense of family, of history, of place; and when Grandma was long gone and I decided to look through the box of pictures in my parents' attic, I found I had not entirely forgotten them. For example, though I had no conscious memory of the picture of children posed in front of a brick schoolhouse, my eyes went directly to one young face, which I knew with certainty belonged to the girl who became my mother. And I could identify the couple in a portrait as "Uncle Charlie and Bertha," though I didn't know their connection to Grandma nor to me. So I asked my mother, and what she could remember I wrote down on the backs of the pictures, which I now keep in the cedar chest my father made for her before they were married.

Also in that cedar chest are black and white photographs of my father's family: some from before he was born; some contact prints he made while a teenager in Montana; some professional portraits; and some he printed himself using the enlarger he put together in the basement of the house where I grew up. Today, in an upstairs closet in my house, are a dozen storage containers of slides, which he began taking about the time I was born. A few years ago I had color prints made from some of these--enough to fill three albums.

So, over the years I have maintained the family connection reinforced by photographs and bedtime stories told by Grandma and by each of my parents. Experts tell us that memories are not facts and that eyewitness accounts often are not accurate. However, I believe that to a large extent we are what we remember. My sense of self today is based on that same sense of self at various stages of becoming who I am. If the following pages focus more on the positive than on the negative, it is because, on reflection, that is how I see my life. I hope that when my life ends I will still feel incredibly grateful. This is what I remember.

4

FAMILY

NOTE: To avoid confusion over identities of the many relatives and friends who appear in what follows, see "Who's Who" at the end of the book.

GRANDMA WARD

Her neck had fine wrinkles and loose folds which hung from her chin, where a few stiff hairs sprouted, to her collar bone. I could not understand why she wanted me to pull out those hairs--I knew it would hurt. Best of all were her hands. She was a big woman for her day--five foot eight--with hands to match. Pushing my own finger into the soft cushion of her fingertip made a depression. She gave me both hands, palms up, so I could make ten dents in a row. My own fingers were disappointing; the flesh persisted in bouncing back.

During the many hours I spent with her, Grandma told me stories about herself. She was born somewhere in Arkansas on March 31, 1872, Easter Sunday. Because of the holiday, they named her Annie Easter. For the rest of her life she corrected people who insisted on calling her Anna Esther. Her father, John Knox, was born in Scotland; her mother, Margaret Bull (a proper Victorian lady who hated her surname), was born in Ireland of Welsh and Scottish ancestry. That was enough for Grandma to consider herself Irish. She loved to listen to Dennis Day sing on the radio. As young adults John Knox and Margaret Bull immigrated separately to Canada, where they met and married. Six children lived to adulthood. Will, the only son, was the oldest; Grandma, the youngest.

When Grandma was two, in 1874, the family traveled by covered wagon from Arkansas to San Francisco. Somewhere along the way, Grandma told me, she fell into a river and was saved by Will, who could swim. She also told how Will died, years later, in the Alaska Gold Rush. He and his partner were paddling a canoe, which I imagined was full of gold, when the canoe capsized. The partner couldn't swim, but Will was able to save him and swim to shore. The partner lived, the gold was lost (I imagined), and Will died of pneumonia. For days, said Grandma, her mother sat rocking at her window, waiting for word from Will, hoping to glance up to see him walking down the street toward her.

After a few years in San Francisco, John Knox, a carpenter, found work in Seattle and filed for a claim sixty miles to the north near the Skagit River and what is now Mount Vernon's Riverside Drive. Grandma and the rest of her family came by steamboat from San Francisco to Seattle, up Puget Sound to Skagit Bay, and up the Skagit River to Skagit City, several miles below Mount Vernon. There, a log jam blocked the river, and the family had to walk from there to their claim. It took all day. Grandma was six years old, and some of the time Will carried her on his shoulders.

Mount Vernon around the time Grandma arrived

Grandma told me all this, and much more, when she took care of me. Sometimes I stayed overnight, sleeping next to her in her double bed. One night when I had a plaster cast on my leg, she woke up to find the leg lying across her chest, but she refused to let me bring to bed the hobby horse Uncle Del made. Out of habit, she kept a chamber pot under her bed, though the bathroom was but a few steps down the hall. A string ran from the light bulb on the bedroom ceiling to the headboard. We could get into bed with the light still on and then turn it out by hooking an arm over the string. I imagined the purple and green wallpaper bouquets in the blackness.

On the claim, Grandma said, Will carved her a boat from a chunk of

6

fir. She was sailing it in a big puddle when the Murray kids came along and told her, "Look, Annie, look at the eagle up in the sky." Grandma told me eagles would carry off small animals and even babies, and eat them. Grandma looked for the eagle but saw nothing. When she looked back at the puddle her boat was gone. The Murray kids said it sank and left, laughing. Grandma got a long stick and felt all around in the puddle but found no boat. Will made her another one. The Murrays were low class.

Among the pictures in Grandma's writing desk was a family portrait of John and Margaret Knox and their grown children; it hangs now on a wall in my home. Seated in the front row with his parents is my Great-Uncle Will. The sisters stand behind them: Aunt Belle, Aunt Siddie (Sarah), Aunt Maggie (Margaret), Grandma, and Aunt Mamie (Mary). The Knox family looks solemnly at me, stylish bangs carefully arranged, moustaches neatly combed, waists tightly corseted; vests, a watch chain, brass buttons, ruffled collars.

Grandma and her sisters about 1941 (from left): Grandma, Aunt Siddie, Aunt Maggie, Aunt Mary, Aunt Belle

I knew all of these great-aunts--some better than others. Grandma was the only sister not to get a divorce. Aunt Belle, the oldest, lived in Canada and died when I was very young. Aunt Siddie had a glass eye. She was flighty, Grandma said. One time when my mother was a baby, Grandma took her and Aunt Siddie for a buggy ride. Grandma drove and Aunt Siddie held baby Hazel, my mother. Suddenly the horse bolted, and Aunt Siddie immediately jumped out with Hazel. When Grandma calmed the horse and drove back she found Aunt Siddie, still holding

Hazel, sitting in a mud puddle, unharmed and incoherent.

Aunt Mamie lived in California and visited occasionally. She had been married three times, once to a captain, and she had a tattoo on her arm. That and the fact that she smoked fascinated me. She also was quite deaf and had a hearing aid the size of a small camera, with a cord running to the earpiece. It squealed a lot of the time, and sometimes she used an ear trumpet instead. It was shaped like a small black saxophone.

Aunt Maggie had a mean streak. As a girl, Grandma got a wax doll whose face looked like real flesh. She kept the doll in a box under her bed and wouldn't let her sister Maggie play with it. One day when Grandma pulled out the box and took off the lid, there lay the beautiful wax doll with a big bite out of her cheek, like a bite out of an apple. As an old lady, sometimes Aunt Maggie wouldn't answer the door, even when she was expecting company.

Grandma had a sideboard, part of the dining room set she got at Denny Dobson's second hand store. Under its flat top were two big doors which opened to the main storage section. When I removed the linens, the silverware, and the crocheted lace tablecloths, there was room to crawl in and lie down with my knees drawn up. As I lay there in the dark I pretended I was in my berth on a train coming home from California after visiting Aunt Mamie and her family, just as Grandma had described. I felt cozy and safe with Grandma nearby, listening to "The Lone Ranger" on the radio, or in the kitchen making lemon meringue pies or getting the stretch candy (taffy) ready for pulling.

In the wide drawer at the bottom of the sideboard was a black cape, which had belonged to my Great-grandma, Margaret Knox. She was Very Religious and wore it to church twice every Sunday. Black beadwork traced patterns of leaves and flowers on the fine satin, and a border of thickly gathered black chiffon ran all along the edges. The cape, which fastened with three large black hooks and eyes, fit perfectly around my waist, making a floor-length skirt. When I put it on I became "Mrs. Flinnigan," Grandma's name for me when I played dress-up and put on airs. Grandma herself didn't go to church, having had more than enough of it as a girl. The family had to row across the Skagit River and back twice each Sunday. Later, though, she joined the Rebekah Lodge, and in her closet were the dresses she had worn to Lodge meetings. One was a floor-length rose beige crepe, with a row of plum-colored sequins lining the neck and wrists. That was the kind of thing Mrs. Flinnigan wore, and I couldn't imagine an old woman wearing it.

Grandma went to bed at nine and rose at five, partly because "Early to bed, early to rise, makes a man healthy, wealthy, and wise," but also because, nearing eighty, she found it impossible to sleep late--her "bones

8

ached," she said. Lying beside her in bed, after she pulled the string to turn out the light, I recited the prayer she taught me, beginning, "Now I lay me down to sleep...." Then Grandma asked God to bless all our living relatives, naming each one, and "all my dear ones in heaven." I thought that when Grandma died she should wear that rosy crepe dress in her coffin. After saying our prayers, she told me more stories from when she was young.

In Grandma's one-room school they used slates and chalk, not pencil and paper. From the beginning they learned to write cursive, with the letters connected, whereas I was first taught to print; writing was not taught until third grade. Not only did she learn to write connecting all the letters, but for special occasions she got to use ink. They didn't have desks, exactly. Instead, the children sat on long benches, and in front of each bench was a long table whose top sloped toward the bench, like the top of a very wide writing desk. Five or six children sat side by side at the table. The old Washington State History Museum used to display a replica of the first schoolhouse in Pierce County, a log cabin measuring about ten by twelve feet. On one side a doorway was cut into the logs, and on the opposite wall was a single four-pane window. A long desk and bench faced the front and the teacher's desk, behind which was the blackboard--literally, a board painted black--like in Grandma's school.

One time she had to memorize a poem to recite before the class. She was afraid she would forget, so she wrote it in the palm of her hand: "In fourteen hundred and ninety-two / Columbus sailed the ocean blue...." The teacher caught her: "Annie, why are you looking at your hand?" She felt foolish, but even more foolish was the little boy she told about, whom the teacher asked to make up a sentence using the word "depot," which she wrote on the blackboard. Finally he said, "At night we put out de cat, turn out de light, and put de pot under de bed."

In summer the children walked to school barefoot, through Douglas fir, cedar, and hemlock. The Skagit River delta was a cedar swamp which farmers gradually cleared by logging and then blasting the stumps with dynamite. Dynamite was not dangerous by itself, Grandma said. The danger was in the blasting caps which set off the dynamite. She told of piles of stumps all over the valley. I dreamed of these stories when I spent the night with her, and in the morning she had my clothes warming by the wood stove.

Grandma saved pennies ("a penny saved is a penny earned") in a round plastic container which she kept on a high shelf in her corner cupboard. Every Christmas I helped her roll the pennies into paper tubes, which we took to the bank and cashed in. The money was mine. Then she began saving pennies again, until the next Christmas. Also in the top part of her corner cupboard were untouchable items of cut and pressed glass, but the bottom of the cupboard was for me: paper dolls, blunt scissors, coloring books, an empty coffee can full of crayons, a Chinese checkers game. In her head were more games: tic tac toe; hide the thimble; button, button, who's got the button; and her favorite, let's see who can be quiet the longest. She had stories, rhymes, and riddles: "Adam and Eve and Pinch Me went down to the river to swim. Adam and Eve were drowned. Who do you think was saved?" Together we looked at the pictures in my glossy Mother Goose book ("Classic Volland Edition") while Grandma recited what her Scottish/Welsh/Irish mother had told her: "To bed, to bed, ya sleepyhead, and dinna be sa slow...."

If I paused and said, "Well...," she would tell me, "A well is a hole in the ground." If I became discouraged I heard, "If at first you don't succeed, suck eggs." Pouting elicited, "Look out or you'll step on your lip." And when I made too much noise she told me to "whisht" as Margaret Knox had told her children in their log house in the woods when Indians, excited by fire water, ran whooping past the windows in the night.

When Grandma was nineteen she married the Grandpa I never knew--Lennie (Lorenzo J.) Ward. As newlyweds they traveled by train to visit his family in Kansas, a place which, she recalled, had more "cleared land" than she had ever seen. During the visit Grandpa's family gave Grandma a pieced star patterned quilt, which she kept but never finished by adding batting and backing. Later my mother had it in a drawer upstairs, and now it is in my closet, still unfinished. Grandma and Grandpa had six children, three of whom died in infancy. My mother, Hazel, was the oldest of those who survived, followed by Claire, and then Mary.

When Grandma was eighty-one and I was twelve she broke her hip. Dr. Ebeling operated to put a pin in her hip. Afterwards, as expected, she went into shock. Mother and Auntie Claire spent the night at the hospital, and I went to bed hoping the phone would not ring in the night, because that would mean Grandma had died. I woke up to daylight, and after that Grandma began, very slowly, to get better. After a while she could sit up in the hospital bed, and then she had to stand and try to walk. Every evening, with one arm over Daddy's shoulders and the other over Nurse Swedene's, Grandma slowly slid her feet down the hospital corridor. Finally she came home to live with us.

Never again could she walk without crutches, and usually someone--mostly my mother, sometimes myself--supported her on one side. I learned to help her to bed, to swing her legs at just the right angle as she lay back, trying to cause as little pain as possible. Grandma was still able to go for rides in the car and to picnics on Whidbey Island or up the River, and she helped at home by sitting in a chair drying the dinner dishes while I washed. Sometimes she could stand at the sink long enough to peel potatoes. She did needlepoint and read magazines and Western novels. When we got television her favorite programs were "Gunsmoke" and Groucho Marx's quiz show, "You Bet Your Life."

At the age of eighty-six after a brief illness they called "quinsy," Grandma died. I was seventeen. I don't remember what she wore in her coffin--just that it was not the rose crepe dress with the plum-colored sequins.

Mom helping Grandma to the car

GRANDPA GRIMES

I don't remember my Grandma Grimes at all, but my mother described her as "a little bit of a thing." There is a picture of my two grandmothers standing together, ready to go shopping downtown. The top of Grandma Grimes' head barely reaches Grandma Ward's shoulder. When I was born my Grimes grandparents lived almost next door, with just a side street and one other house between us. In the only picture of

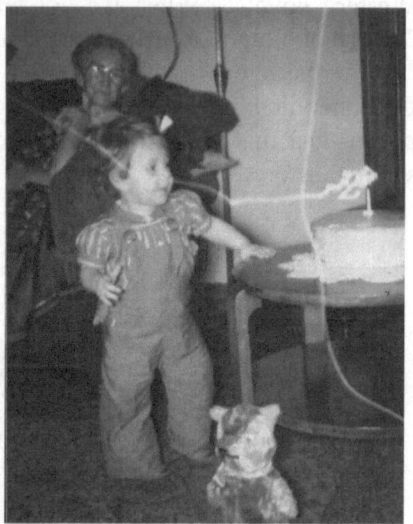

Daddy left the shutter open, causing the yellow streak

Grandma Grimes and me together, I stand at a low table with a pink birthday cake and one candle; she sits on the couch next to the table, looking thin and frail. One month later the Japanese bombed Pearl Harbor, and two months after that Grandma Grimes died.

Since Grandpa Ward and Grandma Grimes were both dead, I thought my living grandparents should get married and suggested as much to Grandma, who wasn't interested. She explained, "He has his life, and I have mine." I didn't ask Grandpa what he thought about my idea. When he died I was just eight years old, and my memories of him are fragmentary.

Grandma and Grandpa Grimes

His most notable physical feature was a raised black thing about the

12

size of a small pea in the middle of his forehead. Grandpa was a carpenter, and I was told that once when he was hammering a nail, the head of it broke off, flew up and embedded itself in his forehead. He was a founding member of Carpenters Union local #954 in Mount Vernon, and served as both business agent and financial secretary until he died. Until the late 1940's, the union local met every Thursday evening at the Labor Temple downtown. Then a new Carpenters Hall was built on the West Side, and a portrait of Grandpa hung in the main meeting room. No other local carpenter was so honored, and the portrait remained until the union was disbanded and the building sold in the 1980's.

Sometimes I was jealous around Grandpa. Ray Bloom was a boy my age whose parents were Aunt Ruth and Uncle Del's best friends. One time Ray and his father were working out in the garage with Del and Grandpa when I heard Ray call him "Jim." I remember thinking, "He's my Grandpa." And when my cousin Kay was born Grandpa thought she was the cutest thing on earth. Kay and I were playing in the front yard one time when Grandpa drove in, and we both ran to see him when he got out of the car. He had bought Kay a new pair of mittens and picked her up and showed them to her. He didn't even notice me.

When Grandpa went to a Carpenters convention in Florida, though, he brought presents back for me and Larry. This was before Kay was born. He handed me a small box, which I opened while he watched. It was full of tissue paper. As I pulled away the tissue and the wad of it got smaller and smaller, it occurred to me that maybe there was nothing but tissue paper--that this might be a joke--and I was afraid I might cry. Grandpa watched and said, "Keep going." Finally I felt something small and hard, and then I saw the present: a Mickey Mouse ring! It glowed in the dark, Grandpa said, and sure enough, when I held the ring to a bright light, then went into a dark place, the ring glowed on my finger. Cousin Larry got a watch which also glowed in the dark.

For Christmas one year Grandpa took the whole family to see the Ice Follies in the Seattle Civic Auditorium. I got out of school in order to go and was thrilled to see so many costumed skaters--like a ballet on ice. For one number the women wore what looked like clear glass skirts--you could see their legs moving around inside. The special number for children featured "Ferdinand the Bull"--on skates!

On Christmas Day 1948, when I was in second grade, we went over to Grandpa's house as usual to open presents from that side of the family. Grandpa sat in the swing rocker looking old and sick. He had trouble opening his presents, and not long after that he had a stroke. When we visited him in the hospital he was feeling better, and I remember sitting beside him on the bed. He came home for a while but then went back to the hospital, and in February 1949 he died. I cried when Mom told me, but Daddy thought I should go to the funeral. We sat behind a screen--I was next to Auntie Ruth, who sniffled and wiped her eyes. After a lot of people walked past the screen on their way out, the family went in to the big room. Daddy lifted me up so I could see Grandpa in his coffin, which got me bawling. Later I told Mom I didn't like funerals, and she said not to tell Daddy because it would make him feel bad.

Grandpa was cremated and wanted his ashes to be scattered over Mt. Baker, which meant Daddy would have to hire a plane. I was excited because I wanted very much to fly in a plane and begged Daddy to take me with him. Since he didn't say no, I was very hopeful until one summer day when I returned from playing and learned he had gone without me. The plane couldn't fly as high as Mt. Baker, so Grandpa's ashes were scattered on Cultus Mountain, which looks down on Big Lake east of town where Grandpa had a cabin.

Later I learned that Grandpa had left no will, meaning that Daddy, Aunt Ruth, and Aunt Carol had to decide how to divide his assets, which amounted to the house on Eleventh Street, the place at Big Lake, and some savings. As far as I know, there were no disagreements in this regard. They split ownership of the Big Lake place three ways; Aunt Ruth got the house in town, where she and her family had lived since 1942; and Daddy and Aunt Carol divided the cash.

I've often wondered if that money enabled us to buy a new car and get rid of the 1935 Ford, shamefully old in my opinion, with running boards and a stick shift on the floor instead of attached to the steering column. That fall, when the new 1950 models came out, I could identify every new car on the road, which amounted to Ford products (Ford, Mercury and Lincoln), GM products (Chevrolet, Pontiac, Oldsmobile, Buick and Cadillac), Chrysler products (Plymouth, Dodge, De Soto, and Chrysler), Studebakers, Hudsons, and Nash Ambassadors. A new Ford custom deluxe four-door sedan in Hawthorne Green was displayed in the showroom when the new cars arrived, and a few days later on a rainy night we picked it up and left the old car, which my Mom called "Lizzie," parked in front of the dealership. I carried Rusty, our red cocker spaniel, to the new car, which I christened "Elizabeth," and put him on the shelf between the back seat and the rear window--his favorite place to ride and finally wide enough for him to fit comfortably. Then we picked up Grandma and took her with us for a short ride.

We drove across the river to the West Side and along some country roads and were on our way home when we stopped for a red light at the Green Gate Tavern in Burlington. Suddenly we were hit from behind and I was knocked off the back seat onto the floor, where I lay sobbing, sure that our wonderful new car was now a pile of junk. Daddy got out to survey the damage and talk to the truck driver who had rear-ended us, and pretty soon he came back smiling. "It's not bad at all," he said, "just a little dent in the bumper." He let me get out and see for myself, and I could hardly believe that big bump had made such a little dent. "I can take the bumper off at home and pound out the dent myself, so you won't even know it's there," he said. And he did. He said now he could relax, the car had been christened, and he wouldn't worry about anything ruining its perfection. I understood his point but still wished the new car had stayed perfect just a little bit longer.

Spitting image of our new 1950 Ford (from internet)

AUNTS AND UNCLES

CLAIRE AND RALPH MARIS

Aunt Claire was born just twenty-two months after my mother, and they were life-long best friends. She was petite, very pretty, and very much a lady, always impeccably dressed, rarely in slacks, with every hair in place. Ladies didn't swear, of course, but when she saw a snake or spider (or suspected one might be in the vicinity) she halfway lost control and cried, "Oh, God-ie!" Because she had no children of her own and loved babies and little children, she doted on me and her only other niece, Barbara. Consequently, she was my favorite aunt. Neither Aunt Claire nor my mother graduated from high school because they got jobs at the telephone office, so why bother? When I was born Mom quit her job, but by then Aunt Claire had worked her way up to Chief Operator, a position she held until she died from breast cancer--too early at age sixty-one.

Aunt Claire and Uncle Ralph (whom I called Roggie) lived in a house just south of downtown on Second Street, which was also Highway 99. Originally the house had two bedrooms, but when it became clear that they couldn't have children, they took down a wall in one bedroom to create a large "L" shaped living/dining room. The kitchen had a breakfast nook. The bedroom dresser held various bottles of perfume, which I liked to finger and carefully remove the stoppers to get a whiff. Auntie Claire had little feet, size five and a half, and by the time I was in third grade her shoes fit me perfectly. When I was about eleven Roggie bought a radio/three speed phonograph: 45, 78 and 33 1/3 rpm. He liked country music, which my father called hillbilly music, but also had other records. I remember recordings of Jeannette MacDonald; the soundtrack from an MGM musical, *Two Weeks with Love*, in which Debbie Reynolds sang "Abba Dabba Honeymoon"; another record featuring an exotic Peruvian singer, Yma Sumac; singles such as "The Three Bells" by the Browns; an hilarious takeoff on a revival meeting called "It's in the Book," which featured a sermon on "Little Bo Peep" and a hymn called "Grandma's Lye Soap."

Their house was just a block from the ball park, home of the Mount Vernon Milkmaids, where there were fireworks after the baseball game on the 4th of July. The first time I saw the fireworks I was very small and had gone to sleep, but Mom had promised to wake me for the spectacle. Nobody realized how the noise would affect me, but at the first big BANG I screamed bloody murder and became hysterical as the noise continued. For years afterward I couldn't watch fireworks without putting my fingers in my ears.

We seemed to do everything with Auntie Claire and Uncle Roggie: picnics, vacations, automobile drives, Sunday dinners, holidays, etc. Sometimes I stayed overnight with Auntie Claire and, because Uncle Roggie had a job as night desk clerk at the President Hotel, I got to sleep with her, which was a big thrill, because she and Roggie were the first people I knew to get an electric blanket. Crawling in between warm sheets was wonderful, but one night I wet the bed, and Auntie Claire woke me up in the middle of the night to change the bedding. That was the only time she got mad at me. We were lucky not to be electrocuted.

When Mom took me downtown she always stopped in at the telephone office to see Auntie Claire and the other "girls" she had worked with before I was born. The operators sat in a long row at the switchboard and wore earphones and devices with speaking tubes strapped to their chests. Auntie Claire would take me in her arms and walk down the row of operators so they could see how much I had grown and could admire my "big brown eyes." They said "number please" over and over and pulled out long cords to plug into the switchboard to make connections. At home, when we lifted the receiver to make a call we heard "number please" instead of a dial tone. One time the operator astonished me when she said, "Thank you, Janet honey."

I used to want blue eyes. Partly this was because strangers often commented on my "big brown eyes." They meant it as a compliment, but instead of being flattered I felt like a freak. The only people I knew with brown eyes were Mom and Auntie Claire. They had gotten their brown eyes from Grandpa Ward, but he was dead. Grandma had blue eyes as did her sisters. Daddy had blue eyes and so did all my other aunts and uncles: Roggie, Ruth and Del, Carol and Howard. and Grandpa Grimes had blue eyes. All my cousins had blue eyes: Bob, Marge, Larry, Kay, Barbara (and her first husband, Dan and son Danny; second husband Curtis; third husband Dick and daughter Beth). The kids in the neighborhood mostly had blue eyes, which isn't surprising considering the northern European make-up of the community at the time. My playmate Joey Kenna's mother admired his "eyes as blue as the sky," whereas mine were brown, like mud. Eventually I came to accept my brown eyes so that years later, when I first read my Dad's comment in a letter written to Aunt Carol when I was six months old, I could laugh. He wrote: "I really think she looks cute but you know how parents are. Probably other people think she is bug eyed."

Uncle Roggie doted on me as much as Auntie Claire. Roggie was a card. He liked to joke and to make kids laugh. Because Auntie Claire was very proper and ladylike, Roggie enjoyed shocking her. He was a belcher and made the most of it:

Roggie: BEL-L-L-C-H!!!

Claire: Ralph! I beg your pardon!

Roggie: BEL-L-L-CH!! Granted!

He had a head of thick, wavy hair, of which he was quite vain. My father, Uncle Del, and Curtis (Barbara's husband) were bald. Roggie told me that all bald men had hair on their chests, because the hair fell off their heads, landed on their chests, and took root there. I halfway believed him, because both Daddy and Curtis had hair on their chests, whereas Roggie had none.

Once when on vacation with Roggie and Aunt Claire, all sleeping in a one-room cabin, Roggie got a small moth in his ear just after the lights were turned off. "Jesus Christ, what's that racket?" Nobody else heard a thing. He got up, looked outside, paced around, grumbled, hollered and made a big fuss in general. Someone finally figured out that he had something in his ear and tried sticking in a Q-tip, to no avail. Then they poured water in his ear, and the moth floated out.

When I was almost twelve I got an autograph book, and Roggie was the first to write in it, on October 13, 1952:

> If you were a little brook and ran away from all my charms
> I would make myself a little dam and hold you in my arms.
> And if you were a Christmas tree and looked down on me my dear,
> I would hang around and thrill you and make you light up every year.-Uncle Ralph (Roggie)

Roggie played the harmonica and the piano and sang hillbilly songs; he bought me a used pair of ice skates when Big Lake froze over in 1949; he took me fishing in a rowboat in Lake Sutherland, where I caught my first fish. He had "gas pains" when he got excited and sometimes when he didn't. The pains were probably angina, for he died of a heart attack when I was thirteen. He had promised me something special for my sixteenth birthday and said he hoped he'd still be around to give it to me. I've always wondered what he had in mind.

RUTH AND DEL VAN SICKLE

My other aunts and uncles were my father's sisters and their husbands: Ruth and Del Van Sickle and Carol and Howard Egan. Since Aunt Ruth and Uncle Del lived just two houses away, I considered their house an extension of my own. Mom would stand on the front porch to watch me safely cross the street so I could go visit Auntie Ruth, who often took care of me when Mom had to go somewhere. I remember playing "elevator" in the kitchen, standing in the triangle of space made

Cowgirl with hobby horse; stick 'em up!

by the open back door and hall door. I had learned about elevators during shopping trips to Seattle. " Ground floor," I would say, opening the doors; then "Going up," crashing them together again. Larry had a little wicker rocking chair which he had outgrown but was just right for me. Once I took it up to the place where the stairway turned. There were two big triangular-shaped steps there rather than a square landing. I put the chair on the upper of these steps and rocked happily until I got too close to the edge and down I came, chair and all. Auntie Ruth rescued me. According to Uncle Del, one time when I was visiting I started bawling for no apparent reason. When asked what I was crying about I replied, "Nothing, I always cry at this time of day."

Uncle Del liked to work with wood. When I became horse crazy, he made hobby horses for me and Kay (who, being younger was horse crazy because I was). There is a picture of me in the backyard astraddle the hobby horse, pointing a cap gun at the camera, and wearing a straw hat and white rain boots--as near as I could come to a cowboy outfit. My jump rope is tied around the neck for reins. Del fashioned the horse's two-dimensional head (in profile) with a jigsaw, and I drew eyes on each side, black circles for nostrils, and lines for the mouth. The body amounted to a sawed-off broomstick with a wheel at the bottom end for easy traveling.

CAROL AND HOWARD EGAN lived in Spokane until I was in high school, so we didn't see them as often as my other aunts and uncles. However, every summer Aunt Carol and cousins Bob and Marge spent two or three weeks in Mount Vernon and stayed at Grandpa's/Auntie Ruth's house. Aunt Carol always remembered my birthday and other special occasions such as Valentine's Day. She gave me books sometimes, and I still have two of my favorites: the first Laura Ingalls Wilder book, *Little House in the Big Woods*, and a collection of stories, *Once There was a King*.

The first time we visited Spokane Grandpa went with us. I was five or six. (Marge would have been eleven or twelve, Bob fourteen or fifteen.) We went in our old 1935 Ford, and it heated up somewhere, maybe on the long hill coming out of Vantage, so we had to stop for it to cool off. We stayed overnight in East Wenatchee with Daddy's cousin and his wife, Archie and Magdalen Rolfs, who had a small farm. To my mother's embarrassment, Rusty chased the chickens as soon as he was out of the car. The oldest Rolfs boy took me with him to feed the cows in the barn and sat me up high so they couldn't get to me, but then he had to leave for a minute, and I started to bawl. He came back right away and was surprised that I might think he would leave me there.

Picking wildflowers with Aunt Carol near Spokane

Continuing to Spokane, we stopped to see the Grand Coulee Dam, which had been built during the Depression and which none of us had seen. I remember the green water sliding over the huge dam, accented with sprays of gushing white water evenly spaced along the top.

20

The Egans had recently moved to a house on Spokane's South Hill at 42 East 27th, and we were slowly driving around the neighborhood looking for the place when we came across Bob and Marge on their bicycles. They led the way while we followed behind in the car. The house had a dial telephone, which fascinated me. It was in a little nook in the hallway, and I sat there a lot and played with the dial until one time when I was doing it the phone rang. It startled me so much I was afraid to play with the phone after that. Every morning across the street a bunch of girls played games on the sidewalk. I watched them from the living room and longed to play with them, but I was too shy to go outside. We went to Natatorium Park, where Bob and Marge got to ride the roller coaster but I had to settle for the merry-go-round, which had a device holding brass rings and one gold ring. If you got a gold ring you got another ride free, but I was too little to reach for a ring, so I only got one ride. I was very interested in houses at the time, intensely curious about floor plans and things like that, and this house impressed me a lot. What I remember especially was Auntie Carol and Uncle Howard's bedroom, which was just off the landing, halfway upstairs.

I was nine or ten when we went to Spokane the second time. We left home on the spur of the moment one afternoon when the thermometer read 98 degrees and got into rush hour traffic in Seattle. I was so hot in the back seat that I took off everything except my underpants. We got to Spokane at midnight, and Auntie Carol and Margie were waiting up for us. That's when I saw a dishwasher for the first time, in Auntie Carol's kitchen. The racks on the inside were round, and I think they whirled around when the machine was turned on. By this time I could swim and got to go in the pool and play on the monkey bars at nearby Comstock Park. I also got to ride a horse one day at a riding academy in the valley. The sorrel horse supposedly was a thoroughbred and a cousin to Seabiscuit, and it was an English saddle so there was nothing to hang onto. It was wonderful!

Marge was in high school by this time, and now she had the room off the landing. I don't know if I was invited into her room, or if I sneaked in when she wasn't around, but I was very impressed with the "high school-ness" of it all. I remember a long string of dance programs (little memento booklets) hanging in a corner. Marge would spend hours on the phone, neither party speaking for long periods of time, until finally one would ask, "Are you still there?" I remember this only because I overheard Daddy mentioning it to Auntie Ruth upon our return. Cly, Marge's best friend, came to dinner once while we were there, and I was struck dumb in the presence of these high school girls. I asked Marge if she had a boy friend, and she said yes, but I didn't see him while we were there. When Marge had a grownup conversation with my Dad about the Ku Klux Klan, which I had never heard of, I was very impressed.

Eventually Uncle Howard's job transferred him to Portland, and on Thanksgiving Day in 1955 we and the Van Sickles (Ruth, Del and Kay) drove down to spend the long weekend with them. Aunt Carol was trying out a new recipe for roasting the turkey, which involved starting it the night before in a very slow oven, and no peeking until it was done. When the lid finally came off all the meat was in the bottom of the pan, with just the skeleton rising above! Aunt Carol never got over her embarrassment, but for the rest of us it became a funny family story.

One summer when I was in college Carol and Howard were living in Seattle (another job transfer) and they invited me to live with them while looking for a summer job there. The Seattle Public Library hired me as a temp, and for three months I commuted via suburban bus from their house in Lake City to downtown. Every morning Aunt Carol got me up at 6:30 with "rise and shine, rise and shine," a line from *The Glass Menagerie,* in which we saw my friend Annaly perform at the UW's Playhouse Theater. Aunt Carol made my lunch for me every day, and during this time I found her to be a true kindred spirit; we shared lots of laughs and became real friends. She had just bought the latest thing, a stereo record player, and I remember listening to LP albums from *My Fair Lady* and *Little Mary Sunshine.*

Most evenings Howard, Carol and I watched TV. It was a very hot, dry summer, and Howard often sat with his bare feet on a footstool directly below my line of sight to the TV. His toenails were long, horny and yellow, which grossed me out to the point that one evening I decided to trim them, which grossed me out even more, but I finished the job, gagging throughout.

I learned to appreciate his wit, best illustrated by the following typewritten letter, dated 6/16/61, which he mailed me in an official Mobil Oil Corporation envelope. It refers to some black and white snapshots I picked up for him in downtown Seattle.

Dear Janet :
In order to enjoy friendly relations with your relations, it is best not to engage in arguments. Especially, when it pertains to money matters. As I recall, we engaged in a heated argument last evening regarding the cost of an item purchased from Bartell Drug Company. I was positive in my own mind as to the cost of the item. However, you were in possession of the receipt, refusing to show me proof of the exact cost. Consequently, I

22

was at your mercy and was forced to accept the amount of money <u>you</u> decided to pay. I'm enclosing the receipt showing the exact amount of money paid out in hopes this proof will spur you on to pay your just obligations.

As you know, I will retire shortly and it is mandatory that I be conservative and watch my pennies. In addition to the money value, my pride is hurt in that a person would discount or doubt my word as to the exact cost of the item.

In case you are unable to meet this obligation at this time I will accept sufficient collateral for a period not to exceed 60 days. No extension of time will be granted beyond this period. There is one other possible solution to this financial problem. We can give you a half of an apple in your lunch. This same procedure would have to be repeated for two more days due to interest charges.

Time is of the essence.

The letter, which I still have, is signed, "Love, Unkie," and stapled to the letter is the receipt, which he retrieved from the wastebasket. It shows a cost of 36 cents, with two cents tax, for a total of 38 cents. He has written "not 36 cents" and circled ".38 total."

COUSINS

BARBARA BREATHOUR

I had five cousins, all of whom were either too old or too young for me to play with except occasionally. The oldest of these was Barbara, daughter of Mom and Aunt Claire's sister Mary, who died of a ruptured appendix when Barbara was in the first grade. Her father wasted no time in marrying Barbara's teacher and making Barbara a second class citizen. So Barbara spent a lot of time with Grandma Ward, my folks, and Claire and Roggie. When I was born Barbara was almost fourteen, so to me she was more like a young aunt than a cousin. She always was with us for holidays and was very much a part of my life. When I was very young two of my favorite things were combing her hair and looking in her purse, both of which she tolerated repeatedly. She graduated from high school in 1945,

With Barbara at the park

when I was four, and I was there, for I remember someone pointing her out as she walked across the platform to receive her diploma. Shortly afterwards, to get away from home, she married Dan Burns, a World War II veteran and sailor, stationed at Whidbey Island. A year after that she had Danny, technically my first cousin once removed, who was almost six years younger than I--again not the right age to play with.

That marriage didn't last long. Barbara and Dan separated, and Barbara got a job working at the Carnation Condensery downtown. During the day Danny stayed at the rooming house at the top of the viaduct where Barbara was living, and the landlady was supposed to take care of him. One day I was with Grandma, walking up the viaduct from downtown to her house on Ninth Street, when we stopped in to see Danny. It was a hot day, and Danny was upstairs alone in a stifling hot room facing west, frantically pacing back and forth in his crib and whimpering. Grandma changed his soaked diaper then and there and told the landlady what she thought. After that Danny stayed at our house with Mom while Barbara was at work, and when she got off work a man in a red Hudson sedan would bring her to pick up Danny. Soon after that Barbara took Danny to California and stayed with Grandma's sister, Great-Aunt Mary (Mamie) and her family for several months until her divorce was final. When she came back she was married to Curtis Graybeal, the man with the red Hudson, and Danny was no longer a baby, but a two-year-old wonder. He could carry a tune and knew a lot of songs, especially Irish and military songs such as "The Halls of Montezuma" and "Anchors Aweigh." He was really smart, and full of the devil. There was talk that he had a genius I.Q, and I asked Daddy if I was a genius. He said no, that I was smart, but I wasn't a genius. For a while I sulked about that.

Curtis was a sheet metal worker and got a job in Bellingham, so they moved up there. Everyone liked Curtis right away, and I was no exception. Before long I was sitting on his lap whenever I got the

At West Beach: Roggie, Aunt Claire, Mom's legs, Barbara, Grandma, myself and Danny on teeter-totter, and Curtis; Daddy's behind the camera

chance--so often that Roggie got jealous and complained that I didn't like him anymore. So then I tried to divide my time between him and Curtis, until finally, several years later, Curtis told me to "get off, Janet, you're too old for that." My feelings were hurt, but of course he was right.

I remember lots of summer Sunday picnics, usually on Whidbey Island, with Barbara, Curtis, Danny, Claire and Roggie, my folks, and Grandma. Sometimes we went to Cranberry Lake or the old ferry landing, but most often the destination was the west side of the narrowest part of the Island, a place we called west beach, now known as Libby Beach Park. At an old, partially burned building we set out the feast on a wooden picnic table: fried chicken, goulash, potato salad, jello with fruit, pie and cake. After lunch we walked the beach, usually to the north, looking for agates, sailing clam shells, and using sticks to hit rocks into the water. There were always dogs, cocker spaniels: our Rusty, Aunt Claire's gold and white Timmy (Timothy McGillicudy, a.k.a Angel Face or Lambikins), and later Barbara and Curtis's black and white Patches. Usually at least one of them found something dead and smelly to roll in.

If we had our picnic at Cranberry Lake, afterwards we would walk a trail, later replaced by a road, along the lake to the beach, all part of Deception Pass State Park. Timmy wasn't the brightest of dogs, and often, while sniffing along off and on the trail, he got turned around and followed our scents back to the picnic area. One of the men had to go find him.

On the way home we always stopped for ice cream cones. Sometimes I had to wear a dress, and once when I went into a cafe with the men to get the ice cream, I sat whirling around on a stool at the counter while waiting. Next thing I knew I was on the floor, my feet were still wrapped around the stool and my skirt over my head. Sailors in one of the booths snickered, and when we got back to the car and Barbara heard about my performance she almost wet her pants laughing. She's never forgotten it.

Back home, everyone came to our house for leftovers. Curtis sat at our kitchen table operating the old toaster with slanted doors on each side. When the doors were opened the toast slid down and flipped over so the other side could toast. It was a responsible job, and once in a while the toast got burned.

Sometimes I was invited to stay overnight with Barbara and Curtis after Thanksgiving or Christmas eve, because they always came back from Bellingham the next day for leftovers, and in the summer I stayed with them for several days or a week at a time. Mostly I just hung around with Barbara shopping or visiting with her "fat friend" Ruth or her "drinkin' friend" Maddy. Sometimes I condescended to play with Danny, which usually ended up with me sitting on him to keep him under control. I helped around the house a little, drying dishes for instance. Barbara said I chipped every piece of her ivy-patterned everyday dishes.

When I was eleven or twelve Curtis was elected secretary for the

26

local sheet metal workers union, and with that office came a portable manual typewriter, which he kept at home. Barbara had taken typing in high school, and she did the actual typing for Curtis.

The machine fascinated me. I hung on Barbara's chair watching her type and finally worked up the courage to ask if I might try. She said okay as long as I was very careful to hit the keys one at a time so as not to jam them. For a couple of days I happily hunted and pecked. When the little bell rang, indicating I was getting close to the end of a line, I carefully moved the carriage return with my left hand in order to continue typing on the next line.

It was the day before I was to go home. Barbara asked me to put the typewriter away and set the table for dinner, so I removed my paper, aligned the carriage so I could close the lid of the carrying case, closed it, grabbed the handle, and swung the case off the table. To my horror, the case opened and the typewriter fell out, landing upside down on the floor. I stared at it, and Barbara rushed over, picked up the typewriter, put it on the table, and tried to type. No luck. The keys only partly moved, and the carriage wouldn't stay in place. I said I wanted a bath, got into the tub, and cried. I'm sure Barbara knew what I was doing. When Curtis came home he had to be told. I went into their bedroom-- the farthest point from the kitchen in their small house. I didn't hear what Curtis said, but I heard Barbara's reply: "You know that you would have let her use it too."

Nothing more was said, but the next day, before I got on the Greyhound bus to go home, Barbara and I took the typewriter to a repair shop, where we learned that the problem, a "sprung carriage," could be repaired. I don't remember the cost, but when I got home Daddy immediately mailed a check to Barbara. I recall no harsh words or scolding. Clearly, I had learned a hard lesson.

For two summers in a row, Curtis was offered a job in Nome, Alaska. Though he would be gone for three months, the job paid a lot, and he accepted. Sometimes I would visit for several days and was old enough now to babysit Danny for a few hours in the evening while Barbara went to a movie with her friend Alice. I didn't want to do it and was sort of scared to be alone at night, except for Danny, who never wanted to go to bed, but it was the price I paid for staying with Barbara. One time I got into my bed on the couch, and before I went to sleep I saw the lights of a car go past very slowly. I sat up to look, and finally the car drove off; but soon it was back, and this time it stopped in front of the house for several minutes before driving off. This repeated itself several more times, and now I was really scared. What if they tried to break in? Would I have time to get to the phone and call the operator?

Or should I get Danny and be ready to run out one door while they broke in through the other? Nothing came of it, but I still wonder what the car was doing.

When I was fourteen and about to start high school, Curtis died suddenly of a massive heart attack. Following just a year after Roggie's death, that ended one phase of my childhood. Once I asked my father what he meant when he referred to "the good old days," a time before I was born. He tried to explain and concluded, "When you grow up, these will be your good old days." Though the period between Curtis's joining our family and Roggie's death was less than six years, they form a large part of my "good old days."

Barbara got married again, to Dick Brannian, and in due course Danny had a half-sibling, Beth. By then I was sixteen--way too old to ever play with Beth, though at times I felt obligated. Barbara's third marriage lasted many years, until Dick's death. Their family was always part of our family gatherings, including Christmas eve, and Barbara always remembered my mother with special flowers on her birthday and at Easter.

LARRY VAN SICKLE

Three of my other cousins (Bob, Marge and Larry) were all six to nine years older than I, and Kay was the same age as Danny, almost six years younger--none of them the right age for me to play with. Larry lived almost next door, but being eight years older he paid little attention to me. An exception was when I accidentally locked myself in the

bathroom at his house. Adults on the other side of the door tried to tell me what to do, but I was crying, and finally they sent Larry to climb in the bathroom window. Just as he got one leg through I unlocked the door myself, much to his disgust.

Larry got scarlet fever one summer, and then Auntie Ruth got it. They were quarantined, and Grandpa and Uncle Del had to live in the cabin at Big Lake like bachelors until the quarantine was lifted. Sometimes they ate with us, and at least once we took dinner to them at Big Lake. Along with neighbors and friends, Mom also sometimes cooked dinner for Larry and Ruth. I went with Daddy to deliver it and had to stand back by the garage while he went to the door and set down the food.

28

Then he backed away and waited for Aunt Ruth to come to the door to get it. They talked briefly, and then we went home. As Larry and Ruth recovered, they worked jigsaw puzzles, and Larry constructed more model airplanes for his collection. When the quarantine was finally lifted, everything in the house had to be fumigated or burned. I remember clothes on hangers on the clothesline. All Larry's model planes had to go, so one by one he set fire to them and sailed them out his upstairs bedroom window.

Just once I remember Larry paid special attention to me. He was in high school by then. We were outside under our kitchen windows on that narrow strip of grass between the house and the driveway, and he was playing with me, throwing me over his shoulder, whirling me around, and apparently enjoying it. Of course, I was thrilled. Then some of his friends drove by in a car and honked, yelling, "Let's go, Larry." When he answered, "Just a minute," I knew he was having fun with me, but soon he left to join his friends.

BOB EGAN

My Spokane cousins, Bob and Marge Egan, were nine and six years older than I was, and they were Catholic because of their father, Uncle Howard. Catholicism was an alien culture in our otherwise Protestant family, almost as strange as Jehovah's Witnesses who stood on street

Bob at the time of his ordination

corners offering "Awake" and "Watchtower" pamphlets. Bob and Marge had to go to church--they called it "mass"--every Sunday no matter what. When they visited Mount Vernon Bob and Larry were inseparable. Of Bob I recall very little from that time, except for one incident. We were all out at Grandpa's cabin at Big Lake, and for some reason the dog, Butch, belched. Someone said. "Butchy belcher," and that sent the two of them into hysterics. They kept drinking water to make themselves belch and saying "Butchy-belcher" and laughing until they fell down.

When Bob graduated from high school in 1949 he declared that he wanted to become a Jesuit priest and went away to Sheridan, Oregon. I didn't see him again until his ordination in 1962. He was very handsome. When Bob first went to Sheridan the Mount Vernon relatives spoke disapprovingly of Bob's vocation. "What a waste," said my mother. At first I had the impression that Bob had renounced the family and that he was no longer my cousin, though Aunt Ruth said, "Why, of course he is," when I mentioned it to her. After he was ordained and living in Seattle, we saw a lot more of Bob. By then Howard and Carol had moved to Mount Vernon. Even my mother accepted him, and he presided at the memorial services for each of my parents.

MARGE EGAN

I adored Marge. Considering our age differences Marge spent a lot of time with me. One of my earliest memories of her and in one of my father's favorite pictures of us together, we are making mud pies at Big Lake. We had all sorts of "molds" such as rusty baking pans, discarded cups, and various bowls. We would scoop the muddy sand into these, drain off as much water as possible, and then turn them upside down on the wooden planks of the dock to dry.

Years later I wrote a poem about Marge and me at Big Lake:

IN THE ROWBOAT AT TWILIGHT WITH MARGIE

At the end of a day of being too little
To swim with Margie and the boys, play board games,
Eat at their table on the porch—
Alone with my mud pies—At last,
Abandoned by the boys, she notices me:
"I'm going out on the lake. Wanna come?"

We glide through reeds, oars dripping,
Groaning softly in their locks, to a
Still place.
A distant cough, a bullfrog, voices
Float around and away;
A fish plops.
Below the ridge, in blackness, the cabin light flickers.
Above, the sky dims from rose to violet. She murmurs:
"Look! The first star."

One time the families (Grimes, Egan, Van Sickle) went to a saltwater beach for a picnic--perhaps somewhere on Whidbey Island. The tide was out, leaving lots of flat, wet sand. Marge decided to draw in the sand a full-size floor plan for a house, while I followed along in open-mouthed admiration. She drew in walls and doorways and windows, and when the house was done we drew furniture into the plan. Then we played house, walking around the rooms, cooking in the kitchen, sleeping in the bedrooms, and visiting in the living room.

Marge always wished she had been named Marsha. When we played house, Marge would be called Marsha. If her paper dolls had names, one would be Marsha. We often played together with paper dolls, though she was almost too old for that. Once I had a new paper doll book which Marge especially liked, and she wanted one for herself. So together we went downtown. I was too young to go alone but was allowed to go with her. And since she didn't know the stores in Mount Vernon very well, my job was to show her where Woolworth's was. Later we were at Auntie Ruth's, playing with our identical paper dolls. (As I recall, this paper doll set consisted of four dolls: two mothers and two daughters, each set having several matching outfits.) My territory was at the bottom of the living room stairs, while Marge's was near the couch. I invited one of Marge's adult paper dolls to come over for tea; we each dressed our doll for the occasion; and when "Marsha" came to visit my doll (probably named Mrs. Flinnigan), they were wearing the same outfits!

Though Marge often condescended to play with me, she wasn't always thrilled to see me. I remember running over to Ruth and Del's early one morning, eager to see the Spokane relatives, especially Margie. She, Bob, and Larry were all still in bed upstairs in the big bedroom, so I ran up the stairs and when Marge saw me she said, "Oh no! It's Janet," and threw the covers over her head. Another time I found her hiding in the berry bushes beside the garage. "Hi Janet," she said without enthusiasm, and continued eating berries.

At Aunt Ruth's house she liked to sit in the plush green swing rocker where she rocked back and forth, banging her head hard on the high back, for long periods of time. I might not remember this except for the fact that the adults often commented on it. I tried it myself once or twice but couldn't discover her fascination; besides, I was a little afraid that if I banged too hard, I'd fall over backwards.

One particular time Marge discovered a new kind of "goooood peanut butter" which Aunt Ruth had bought. I kept hanging around until she offered to make me a sandwich. Though I wasn't hungry, I was not about to refuse any favor offered by Marge. The trouble was, she didn't put any jam on the sandwich, and to me it was dry and tasteless. So after taking a bite or two I decided to take the sandwich home and threw it in the gutter on the way. Later I went back, and after a bit Marge decided to go over to our house to play the organ. We crossed Section Street, and there in the gutter lay the remains of my sandwich. "Janet!" she said. "Is that your sandwich?" "No," I lied. "Yes it is! And that goooood peanut butter!"

One day during our second visit to Spokane Marge put on her oldest jeans because she had to paint the metal lawn chair. I watched her apply a bright red enamel oil-based paint (this was before the invention of acrylics), and when she was finished she warned me not to sit in the chair, and I didn't--then. I waited until the paint was partly dried and I had forgotten all about the chair being freshly painted. I can still feel the sticky, slippery paint on my bare legs and arms. I had on shorts and a T-shirt, and they got it too. I remember standing naked on newspapers while Mom and Aunt Carol swabbed me with paint thinner. Whether or not the clothes survived, I don't know. And Marge was particularly disgusted because she had to repaint the chair to remove my body print.

There was one more reason I'm sure Marge was happy to see us go home after this visit. By this time I had taken a year or two of piano

32

lessons and discovered some piano sheet music with a simplified version of "The Halls of Montezuma" which I found especially rousing. I played it over and over, until finally Marge hid the music.

On July 4, 1950 I witnessed the firecracker episode at Big Lake. We didn't arrive until after Marge had dared Larry to throw her in the lake, and he did (fully clothed). When we got there Marge was dried off and wearing a new fashion she called "red jeans," what later became known as "pedal pushers"--pants that ended just below the knee. Larry was there with his girl friend, Pat. They and Marge were lighting firecrackers--the ones about the size of your little finger--with punks. Marge had put a handful of them in the pocket of her red jeans, and later she absentmindedly stuck her punk in the same pocket. Suddenly a lot of firecrackers went off all at once, and Marge was screaming and jumping around doing a crazy dance. Several adults helped her, crying and no doubt in shock, back to the cabin and into the bedroom. Aunt Carol, probably in shock herself, asked Marge, "Are you hurt?" Marge sobbed, "Oh no, it happens every day!" There were a lot of women in the bedroom and also my Dad, and I squeezed in and watched Marge take off her ruined red jeans and then her underpants (not even caring that Daddy was watching, I noted). There were a number of nickel-sized holes in the flesh of her upper thigh, where the pocket had been. At the hospital in Mt. Vernon Dr. Ebeling gave her a tetanus shot, cleaned the wounds, and kept her overnight. The next day she was back at Auntie Ruth's, sadder and wiser.

A year or two later, again while Marge was visiting during the summer, I ran over to Auntie Ruth's after breakfast. Marge was in the swing rocker, softly banging her head. A wide piece of adhesive tape lay across the bridge of her nose. "What happened to you?" I asked. "I was in a wreck," she said, and kept rocking. She had been with some other teenagers, probably including Sharon Baxter, and the car had taken a corner too fast and rolled. Later when I learned that Marge was now smoking I suspected that the wreck and firecracker incidents were God's way of punishing her, trying to get her to shape up and live a clean life.

KAY VAN SICKLE

Kay was born to Aunt Ruth and Uncle Del just a couple of months after Barbara had Danny, when I was almost six. Once again, a cousin the wrong age for me to play with. However, I loved to run over and watch Auntie Ruth bathe her and get her ready for the day. She had enough dark brown hair for Ruth to wet and comb over one finger to make a little sausage curl on top of her head. Most of the time, though, I thought Kay got way too much attention.

By the time she was walking and talking I considered her something of a pest, like Danny, though not as rambunctious. Secretly I wanted her to adore me the way I adored Margie, but I don't think she ever did, partly because I was around all the time. Like me, Kay adored Margie, whose visits were infrequent and therefore special.

For want of anyone my age, I sometimes played with Kay, pushing her in her swing or entertaining her by climbing the cherry tree and hanging by my knees. When I got older, in fifth and sixth grades, I babysat for her when her folks and mine went to Carpenters meetings and when Ruth and Del went square dancing. I had recently learned "the facts of life" and was fascinated by the mechanics of how egg and sperm get together; I had to share it with somebody. Kay was handy, and I drew a diagram of the ovaries, fallopian tubes, and uterus and explained the whole process to her. She acted interested, but soon afterwards Aunt Ruth told me Kay was too young to understand and not to continue with that. I didn't mind babysitting for her; I got paid and she went to bed without too much fuss. But I wasn't comfortable alone with just Kay in the house. This was before television, and I must have brought something to read, but I didn't like sitting in the living room with the shades up when it was dark outside. Somebody might walk by and see

Being nice to Kay for a change

34

me alone in there. I was afraid to close the shades because I would have to be right in front of the windows and would be fully exposed if someone were watching. Also, when Ruth and Del got home they would ask why the shades were down and wonder if I was afraid, which I didn't want to admit.

Sometimes I wasn't very nice to Kay. One summer day when the Traunum girls had a pup tent set up in their back yard across the alley, Nancy and I were lying in it not doing much. Then I saw Kay, who was about three, come toddling down the alley, and Nancy and I pretended to be asleep. Kay came to the tent's opening, crawled in part way, and said, "Jan?" We ignored her. She walked around the tent saying "Jan?" and "Nan?" getting no response. Finally she went home.

I teased Kay, partly to see how far I could go. For instance, when I was studying genetics in high school biology I told her she would be bald when she grew up. I explained about dominant and recessive traits, such as baldness. Since her father was bald and so were my father (her uncle) and our grandfather, there was baldness on both sides of her family. Therefore, she was bound to be bald. Later I learned that she worried about this for a long time.

Once she came over to our house when I was eating a piece of cake. She looked at it longingly but knew better than to directly ask for some. "I sure wish I had a piece of cake," she said. Perversely, I thought if she wanted some cake she should ask for it and not hint. Maybe I eventually broke down and offered her some. But maybe not. I thought she was spoiled and got whatever she wanted, so occasional deprivation would serve her right. This might be one reason Kay says she used to be afraid of me.

She came over when I had the mumps and Grandma was alone with me. Kay wasn't supposed to come in, but Grandma couldn't keep her out. Soon after she came down with the mumps herself and shared it with Larry and Aunt Ruth.

To sum up, while I was always very interested in Kay, she was around all the time and therefore often annoying, almost like a younger sibling. Too bad I wasn't as nice to her as my older cousins, Barbara and Marge, were to me.

OTHER RELATIVES

WINIFRED

Winifred was Mom's cousin, daughter of Uncle Garrie and Great-Aunt Mary (Grandma's sister), who all lived in Palo Alto, California. Before I met Win I felt I knew her. We talked on the phone a few times when the family gathered on a Sunday afternoon to place a long distance call. And I wrote her letters in big capitals, dictated by Mom: D E A R ("skip a space") W I N etc. She had a business in San Francisco with her father, Uncle Garrie, called The Natalie Shop, which sold knick-knacks and trinkets. Sometimes Win sent me presents from the store: a box of Christmas cards (little angels ascending a staircase), a pottery cup with my name on it, a Mr. Potato Head kit from the Miles Kimball Co., which for years afterward sent me their catalogs. Once, for Easter, Win sent me two dresses--a white one in dotted Swiss, and a lacy blue one with a delicate flower pattern.

I finally met Win for the first time when I was four or five. Grandma and Auntie Claire had taken the train to California to visit, and Roggie planned to drive down and bring them back. It wasn't until the night before that my parents told me we were to go with him. At the time the farthest I had ever been from home was Wenatchee and Vancouver, BC. Before the trip to Vancouver I identified myself by stating my name, address, and phone number, adding mournfully, "never been out of the state in my life."

I was so excited about going to California that I threw up intermittently until the wee hours. Mom and I were in the kitchen, where she gave me a cup of hot water to try to settle my stomach, when the phone rang. It was Roggie, who couldn't sleep either and knew me well enough to guess my condition. And so, at two-thirty in the morning we all set out for California.

I remember driving through downtown Seattle with no traffic, lots of red dirt along the highway as we drove through Northern California, and being carsick most of the way. When we crossed the Golden Gate bridge, however, I was asleep. In Palo Alto Mom, Daddy and I waited on the sidewalk behind a hedge while Roggie went alone to the door. I heard Auntie Claire say, "Why, it's my husband!" Inside, Grandma (as she told me later) thought, "Oh darn, Janet didn't come." Then she heard me giggle, and all of us were welcomed into the big living room. I kissed Grandma and Auntie Claire, then ran to Win's open arms.

For the next few days I was treated like a little princess. Win called me "Darling Janet," and I followed her everywhere. She sat beside me at fancy restaurants and kept me entertained, and she told me bedtime stories about a flying horse named Pegasus, which I envisioned as the Mobil gas emblem, the flying red horse. On Easter Sunday the Easter Bunny left colored eggs in the back yard, where Win helped me find them.

Carsickness was a small price to pay for discovering that Winifred was every bit as wonderful as I had imagined, and for getting to see for myself that wonderland I had heard so much about: California!

ALICE AND CHARLIE

Mom's cousin Alice Kennedy and her husband Charlie moved from Missouri to Burlington, just three miles away, when I was about six and they were in their sixties. They were childless, and years later Mom told me with a smile that Alice suspected this was because Charlie put something in her coffee. I thought Alice and Charlie were the two dullest people on earth, largely because of visiting them with the family (Auntie Claire and Roggie, my folks, and Grandma). Their house had few things to amuse me, and for some reason I never brought anything from home to play with--maybe

Alice and Charlie with Grandma, Daddy, myself and Rusty, on the dock at Big Lake

Mom thought it would be rude. So there I sat, listening to Alice drone on about relatives I'd never heard of, trying to figure out if Buster's daughter had been born before or after Norma's second son.

For a while I could amuse myself watching Charlie's nose and Alice's eye. Charlie's nose was unusually large, covered with very large pores like little dimples. I thought of his nose as three flesh-colored strawberries: a big strawberry in the middle with smaller strawberries surrounding the nostrils on each side. Charlie was very tall and had little to say. Alice was fairly tall herself and had a wandering eye (blue, of course). One eye would be looking at you while the other was searching the wall over yonder. If I asked her, she would touch her nose with the tip of her tongue, an accomplishment I envied and never mastered. Perhaps her tongue was especially long because of all the exercise it got.

After spending a respectable amount of time studying Alice's eye, Charlie's nose, the wallpaper with big globs of flowers, and the faded reproductions in ornate frames, I was permitted to walk from one end of the house to the other. It was constructed like a train with a few sidecars. First was the living room, with a door to one side leading to Alice's bedroom; beyond the living room was the big dining room with the oil burner, which heated the entire house, and a side door (sometimes closed) to Charlie's bedroom. Next came the little dining room, one step down from the big dining room. It had a linoleum floor, a small table and chairs, and was painted a blinding yellow. Off the little dining room was the bathroom, which I visited more than I needed to just for something to do. The last room was the kitchen.

Back in the living room after this round-trip journey, I had three options: sit down and continue listening to Alice talk while studying her eye and Charlie's nose; persuade Daddy or Roggie to play Chinese checkers with me; or play by myself with The Toy. I vaguely recall that Charlie acquired The Toy somehow through his insurance business. It was a wind-up device--a jointed plastic girl, attached by her hands to a metal bar. As the spring wound down, the girl flipped and contorted herself over and under the bar. This had to amuse me until I became old enough to stay home by myself rather than visit Alice and Charlie.

Periodically they drove down from Burlington to visit with Mom and Grandma, who by then was living with us. Charlie had a gray 1947 Oldsmobile, the first car I ever saw with automatic (sort of) transmission. When I walked home from school and saw their car was parked in front of the house my heart sank, but at least at home I could escape. After saying hello and giving Alice a kiss (she always smelled like Avon's "To a Wild Rose" cologne) I would announce that I had to do my homework and go upstairs to my room where I read movie magazines and played records until Alice and Charlie went home.

I have always felt a little guilty about my attitude toward Alice and Charlie. They were kindly people, never anything but pleasant toward me. When I needed a trunk to ship things to graduate school in Ohio, Charlie hauled down a big trunk from the attic and gave it to me. He said he had another trunk if I needed it. Even then, he knew he was dying of colon cancer. Alice lived quite a few years longer, with an increasingly serious heart condition. Whenever she wasn't going to a niece or nephew's home for Christmas eve, she came to our house. There is an old slide Daddy took, a portrait of Alice with our Christmas tree in the background. She's resting her face in one hand, her eyes wandering in different directions, looking for happier Christmases past. It almost makes me cry.

AUNT SIDDIE

Her real name was Sarah Perkinson, the youngest of Grandma's four older sisters. She had worked as a midwife and as a cook for prospectors during the Alaska Gold Rush, was divorced from a "no good man" and had one son, Ray, older than my mother.

When I knew her Aunt Siddie was an invalid because of a massive infection which had settled as boils under an arm and near one eye. The doctor didn't know what the trouble was, and when another doctor was called in the damage was done. He drained "a quart of pus," Grandma told me, from under Aunt Siddie's arm, and more pus from her eye. From then on she couldn't use her arm, and what remained of her eye had to be surgically removed, replaced with a glass eye.

Though she lived with her son's family for a while, and with Grandma when she lived by the grain elevator at the bottom of the hill, I remember her mainly from when she lived in Burlington at Mrs. Burton's, now The Burton Home. This was when I was five or six, and Grandma lived on South Second Street next to Coca Cola bottling works. Second Street was also Highway 99, and the bus from Seattle ran past on its way to the depot downtown. Grandma and I would cross the street and wait to flag down the bus so we could ride to Burlington and visit Aunt Siddie.

After stopping at the depot the bus continued north. Sometimes Aunt Maggie, Grandma's next older sister, joined us, getting on where the Highway passed near her house north of downtown. We had hardly sat down before we got to Burlington where we got off, and the bus continued north to Bellingham.

We walked a few blocks down the main street, past the Rio Theater where, a few years later, I saw Walt Disney's *Cinderella*; then we continued beyond the business district to Mrs. Burton's--an ordinary house in a neighborhood. Aunt Siddie and a dozen or so old people, mostly women, lived there. If Aunt Siddie was not feeling well she would be in bed in the room she shared with another old woman. Otherwise she and the other residents sat around in the living room with the visitors. Nobody said much. It was summer and hot, with the windows open but the shades down and flapping in the slight breeze. That was the only sound.

Fortunately, we didn't stay long. Grandma, Aunt Maggie and I would kiss Aunt Siddie goodbye and walk back through town to Highway 99 to wait for the southbound bus from Bellingham. Usually Grandma and Aunt Maggie wiped away a tear or two.

UNCLE ED AND NINA

Uncle Ed, my father's uncle, was a man of many talents, including photography and music. When I was two he took a picture of my folks and me in front of the Christmas tree. I swear I remember this, because he set up the camera on a tripod, said "Watch the birdie," and pulled some kind of toy bird out of his pocket and held it up for me to look at. In the picture, I'm laughing.

He had perfect pitch, and after we got a piano he regularly came over to tune it with his tuning fork, an instrument with a thin handle and two prongs. When struck, the two prongs vibrated a certain tone, and Uncle Ed would cock his head to listen and then adjust each piano key by tightening or loosening the wires inside the piano, so that its tone was

40

correct in relation to the tuning fork.

According to others in our family, Uncle Ed's wife, Nina, was "different." As a child I was unaware of what made her different, except that she didn't like animals and would not let their son, Jimmy, have a dog. When I was small Ed and Nina lived next door, and I used to go "visiting" for five minutes, the time limit Mom set. One time Peggy, our dog, followed me and sat on the porch until Nina noticed her and told her to "siccum." Another time I found Nina in bed. She announced that she was sick and had vomited. "What?" I asked. It was a new word. "I threw up," she explained. Never one to take a hint, I probably had to be told to go home. Her Christmas presents were practical items such as a box of Kleenex. Nina was very thrifty and was known to walk downtown just to deposit a quarter in the bank. Before they moved, she liked to take me with her to visit her sister Alice Alvord, who lived several blocks away. Alice had a daughter, Leslie, about three years younger than I, and Alice always gave Leslie and me a special treat, a single square from a Hershey bar. It amazed me that Alice thought such a skimpy amount of chocolate was anything special, but I had to act pleased.

To be fair, I should mention some nice things about Nina. I still have the pink and white quilt, with animals embroidered in blue, that she made for my crib. And one Christmas eve when the doorbell rang I was told to see who was there. Sitting on the porch was a rag doll bigger than I was, with hair of yellow yarn and embroidered features on her face, which Nina had made for me. But as Uncle Del once said, she didn't know how to have a good time. When I was twenty-one I sat beside Nina for three hours in a Spokane church where my cousin Bob was ordained Father Robert Egan, S.J. Each person was given a booklet in Latin and English to help follow along during the ceremony. In the middle of this, when a bell rang, Nina suddenly thought of something. "I've got to remember to wash out my hose tonight," she told me.

Ed and Nina, Ruth and Del, Grandpa and my folks all lived on Lincoln Hill, where the soil was poor--mostly clay. So during the War they went together and rented a plot of land for a Victory Garden to raise vegetables. I remember the corn especially. The garden was just below the hill, between the railroad tracks to the west and a distinctive large white farmhouse to the east. On its second floor was a balcony with large curved wooden pieces like ornate parentheses at either end. I just ran around and played while the grownups worked in the garden. Occasionally a train, pulled by a steam locomotive, came by.

When Ed and Nina moved to the West Side, there was enough room for a big garden for all of us. They built a nice big house, and the family was invited over for dinner on occasion. Nina served us on paper plates. The new house had a full basement, with a player piano whose keys moved by themselves, controlled by a white scroll with holes in it, which unwound systematically. Uncle Ed also played the guitar and sang silly songs, such as "Big Chief," which I later realized was racist. It went like this:

Big Chief Beela Boola Bungaloo
Came here to be a slave.
Shanghaied by a wily Yankee crew,
Oh, how that man did rave.
By and by all those yellow wenches wanted to take his hand.
Why he would not marry they could never understand.
Big Chief, noble birth, didn't want to marry every girl on earth;
So at last he said in accents rending:
"In Zulu land, there's a Kickapoo lady,
In castle grand, by the foliage green,
I won her hand. Keep a tippin' your katy,
All understand, she's my Kickapoo queen."

Soon after moving to the West Side, Uncle Ed bought a radio-phonograph which could make recordings. When a special phonograph needle was set on a plastic disk--like a small record but without grooves--and Uncle Ed turned a switch, the needle cut into the blank disk, recording whatever sound the microphone picked up. As grooves were cut, a thread of plastic curled away from the needle, creating a loose ball of plastic thread when the process ended. Each side of the record lasted three to five minutes at most.

Uncle Ed told me if I sang a song he would record it and play it back so I could hear it. I was in second grade, and my favorite song our class learned from the music teacher was "Nelly Bly." He set everything up, and when he started to record I developed stage fright. The first side of the record consisted of whimpering, crying, and whining "I can't!" while other voices tried to encourage me. I watched the needle move closer and closer to the record's center as the ball of plastic thread increased in size. Finally side one was finished. Uncle Ed turned the disk over, and I tried again. More crying and whimpering until finally, with barely enough time left, I sang the whole song. Having broken the ice, I knew that someday I would be a star.

A couple of years later, when I was in fourth grade, the Van Sickle and Grimes families gathered at Ed and Nina's on New Year's Day 1951. Since the Egans were in Spokane, Uncle Ed decided to make a record for them. After everybody said hello, I played some Christmas carols on my flutophone, no longer intimidated by the microphone. Then Kay and I sang "Rudolph the Red Nosed Reindeer," with Kay chiming in about a half measure behind me. Then Daddy played the guitar while he, Uncle Ed and some of the others sang.

Sometime after that Uncle Ed had a stroke and spent the rest of his life, five or six years I'd guess, in bed, either in a nursing home or at home with Nina or a part-time care-giver. He couldn't talk much, and he cried whenever family members visited him. Years later I learned more about the stroke from Aunt Ruth, who told me he had come home one night, staggered around in the kitchen, fell down and couldn't get up. Nina thought he was drunk, though to my knowledge he wasn't a drinker, and went to bed, leaving him on the floor. When he was still there the next morning she realized he might not be drunk. By then, not much could be done for him.

The last time I saw Uncle Ed he was in bed at home, and Daddy told me to go into his room because it would probably be my last chance to

see him. I didn't want to, but I did, to please my father. Mom told me later that when she kissed Uncle Ed he mumbled, "Everybody needs love," as tears rolled down his cheeks. He died in 1958.

Because they had loved Uncle Ed, the family still included Nina in many family gatherings. And when Ruth was the only one left of her generation, and Nina lay in a nursing home demented, curled in a fetal position, Aunt Ruth still visited her regularly, because Nina was family, the widow of her dear Uncle Ed.

43

WORRY WARTS

I come from a family of worry warts on both sides. Daddy tended to worry about a wide range of things, including those out of his control such as the state of the globe and disrespectful individuals. His attitude was: prepare for the worst; then, if it doesn't happen, it's a pleasant surprise. When traveling he refused to make reservations and then worried all day about maybe not finding a place to sleep that night. As for his worries about me, they tended to involves fears for my character development ("sigh--I don't know how she'll turn out").

My mother and Grandma worried primarily about my physical well being. "Don't let the Boogyman get you," Grandma warned. Any time I left the house Mom's parting words were, "Have you gone to the bathroom?" and "Be careful." She was still saying this when I was over forty.

Everybody worried out loud: "I've never felt like this before--I wonder if I might have polio" (Daddy). "They should be here by now. I hope they haven't been in a car wreck--but maybe they've just had a puncture" (Grandma). "Remember to thank Mrs. Peterson, and BE CAREFUL" (Mom).

This environment, along with inherited worry genes, culminated when I was in fourth grade. Mom, Dad, Claire and Roggie had gone to Seattle for the day while I stayed with Grandma. When they hadn't returned by the time I thought they should I began to worry. The fear built, and though Grandma tried to distract me with a game of Chinese checkers, I was out of control, skidding down the steep slope of imagined disasters. "Why don't they come? Why?" I wrung my hands, cried, paced the floor. When they finally showed up at a perfectly reasonable hour I was a wreck and so was Grandma.

And that was just the beginning. I wasn't afraid to go places without a parent so long as I knew at least one of them was at home. But I couldn't tolerate being separated if I didn't know how to reach them. One night when I was spending the night at my friend Nancy's, I wanted to check to be sure my folks were home. No one answered the phone. I called Grandma's house, but she didn't know where they were. Auntie Claire and Roggie didn't answer. Maybe they were with my folks; maybe all of them had been in a wreck. By the time I located them I was hysterical. They came and took me home, but in the middle of the night I threw up. It wasn't the flu, because I was fine the next day.

Every other Thursday I stayed overnight with Grandma while Mom and Dad went to the Carpenters and Ladies Auxiliary meetings. Grandma and I always went to bed at 9 o'clock, but one Thursday I couldn't go to sleep for wondering if my folks were home yet. Finally I insisted on calling home, and when I got no answer I panicked. I couldn't rest until I knew they were safe at home. Against Grandma's wishes, I called the Carpenters' Hall and asked for Forrest Grimes. I begged him to come get me. He did, but he wasn't happy about it. He drove back to the Hall, and I had to sit in the car in my pajamas until he and Mom were ready to come out.

After that I didn't spend the night with Grandma anymore. When my folks went to Carpenters they took me to Auntie Claire's and picked me up on the way home. I was persuaded not to worry until ten o'clock, and they always arrived before the witching hour. Gradually, I learned to control my fears, and by fifth grade I was pretty much back to normal. Eventually I was paid to babysit Kay so Ruth and Del could go to the meeting. Having that responsibility helped also.

Years later Aunt Ruth told me that Kay had gone through the same experience. I asked how Kay had gotten over it. Ruth said that I had talked to Kay about my own experience, and that had reassured her and helped her begin to recover. So I guess I did something nice for Kay after all.

CHRISTMAS

My first Christmas was spent crying from colic. The next few Christmases I spent throwing up due to excitement. By the time I started school I was calm enough to enjoy the festivities.

I didn't believe in Santa Claus. This was my father's idea, to spare me the keen disappointment he had experienced when he discovered it was all a sham. Though his purpose was noble, it backfired. From my point of view, all the other kids got stuff from Santa, but I just got stuff from family! Nevertheless, for several years I went through the ritual of sitting on Santa's knee and telling him what I wanted him to bring me. As a small child, I could never think of what to ask for, but at Grandma's suggestion I asked for "a candy cane and a dolly." I didn't care much for dolls (except for the Didy-Doll that wet its pants) and hated the peppermint taste of candy canes. One Christmas I got one about three feet long. For weeks my mother hacked off pieces of that thing and passed them around after dinner—a poor excuse for dessert!

On Christmas eve we opened presents from Mom's side of the family, who came to our house; this included nine or ten human beings and two to three Cocker Spaniels. Christmas morning we walked half a block to Grandpa's/Aunt Ruth's house to open presents from Dad's side of the family. I always wished I could get all my presents at once so I could admire my stash in one great heap instead of two smaller ones. Later that day Mom's side came back for Christmas dinner at our house. Dad mixed up the Tom & Jerrys (with Four Roses whiskey and much fussing over the batter) before we sat down to shrimp cocktail, turkey,

46

giblet gravy, dressing, mashed potatoes, sweet potatoes, pickles, olives, cranberries, various vegetable side dishes (including green beans mixed with cream of mushroom soup and fried onion rings on the top), and mince (ugh!) and pumpkin pie with real whipped cream beaten by hand—often my own.

It was my job to make a decorative arrangement on the piano, starting with a roll of white cotton and a mirror, which became a lake surrounded by a snowy landscape. To this I added Santa in his sleigh, a plastic snowman, small angel and choir-boy candles—whatever seemed appropriate--and finished by sprinkling ivory flakes over it all.

The first present I remember giving was to my mother, who wanted

a compact. Dad took me to Stewart's Drug Store to look at the selections displayed in a glass case. I knew immediately which one I wanted: the biggest, heaviest, gaudiest of a dozen or so. It was about 4 inches square, with a picture of a big pink cabbage rose under glass on the lid. When Mom opened it she "oooed and ahhhed" appropriately, but she never used it. Eventually I figured out why!

Another time I got her a Better Homes and Gardens cook book (an item on her wish list). I was so excited I couldn't help dropping hints, never expecting her to guess, and she played along. Just as the first relatives drove up on Christmas Eve I gave her one last hint: "Mom, your cook book starts with C." She tried not to laugh, and I burst into tears.

Many of my gifts were practical: a white wool blanket for my bed, bubble bath, stationery, clothing, seven pairs of underpants (each embroidered with a different day of the week), a Bible. Others were not so practical, such as storybook dolls that came in cardboard boxes covered with big polka dots in various colors. During a certain period there were horse statuettes, Roy Rogers stuff (a blue shirt with fringe, cowboy pants, a holster with six-shooters, and an alarm clock with Roy astride Trigger—who galloped every time the clock ticked). Later on came Jantzen sweaters and record albums (often movie musical soundtracks such as *Oklahoma! Carousel, My Fair Lady, Camelot, Gigi, The King and I*).

Because our house was small, so was the Christmas tree, often sitting on a little round table to save space and keep the dogs from getting into it. Once the relatives arrived with their presents the area surrounding it was so heaped with packages that the tree seemed to grow out of the pile. Sometimes we hung silvery icicles among the ornaments, but other times Daddy took the tree down the basement and "flocked" it, using an aerosol spray that looked like snow on the branches.

Grandma, Claire, Mom, Roggie, me, Danny

Hijacking Danny's fire truck while Roggie rings the bell; in background--Grandma, Aunt Claire, Mom

Christmases were seldom white, but I remember one when my cousin Kay and I were both grown. After stuffing ourselves at dinner we went outside to make a snowman. It ended up being a very artistic Husky dog, lying down with its head raised. We had trouble with the muzzle until one of us got an old spoon to use as rebar. We were inside warming up, looking outside at our handiwork, when a live dog came trotting down the sidewalk. It spied our Husky, sniffed it all over, and calmly lifted its leg, giving the Husky a yellow face.

ENVIRONMENT

THE HOUSE

When I was born the house had a main floor, a half-basement, and an unfinished second floor. My father drew up the plans and started building it before he and my mother got married on August 6, 1929. The original plan called for a main floor, a half-basement, and an attic. When the newlyweds returned from their  honeymoon car-camping on the Olympic Peninsula, they discovered that Grandpa Grimes and Uncle Ed had framed up a second story. Grandpa, anticipating an expanding family, told my father he would be glad of it later, but Daddy kind of resented having his plans tampered with. Eleven Depression years passed before Grandpa was vindicated, when I arrived on November 8, 1940. Another seven years passed before the upstairs was finally finished and we began sleeping there. Until then, we lived on the main floor, with kitchen, dining room, living room, bathroom, hall, and one bedroom. On the south side of the kitchen were the sink, cupboards, drawers, and drain boards (sloping sections of the counters on each side of the sink, where washed dishes could drain before drying with dish cloths). In my early childhood the windows above the sink were filled with my mother's cactus plants. Later these gave way to African violets, which overflowed into the dining room and main floor bedroom. Beneath the counters were drawers, more cupboards, and two bins--one for flour, the other for sugar. The bins were hinged at the bottom, with handles at the top, just under the counter. Mom emptied big cloth sacks of sugar and flour into the bins; then, when she was baking, she pulled the bins open and scooped out flour or sugar as needed. The cloth sacks she saved and made into dish towels. Later Daddy replaced the bins with more drawers.

Opposite the kitchen windows was a doorway to the hall. I remember Daddy coming home from work still in his overalls and lifting me high above his head until I could touch the top of that door frame. On the left side of the doorway were the stove and trash burner. When my parents first moved into the house in the spring of 1930 only the kitchen, hall, bathroom and bedroom were finished. Doors shut off the unfinished living and dining rooms, and the trash burner was their only source of heat and hot water. After they got a coal furnace, the trash burner, lit in the morning and again after supper, was enough to keep the house comfortable on a warm spring or fall day. When I got up on chilly mornings I sat in the corner next to the trash burner where Daddy had lit a fire with newspaper and kindling.

A wall telephone and a built-in device were on the other side of the doorway from the stove and trash burner. The built-in consisted of a three-piece folding table and an ironing board which could rest on top of the folded table. The whole business folded into a giant, flat cupboard in the wall when Mom scrubbed the floor. Usually the table was open, with just enough room for the three of us to sit for a meal: Daddy on the far side, Mom opposite him with her back to the stove, and me at the end or, even earlier, at the corner by Mom, so she could supervise.

One end of the kitchen led to the dining room. On the little ledge above the door frame lay a wooden yardstick, compliments of Masser's Lumber Company. Occasionally it was used to measure something. However, from my point of view it served as a threat. The yardstick was an instrument of punishment, to be used on me. I have no recollection that it ever was used for that, though perhaps it was the time I clobbered Judy Fairman with the mallet from my pegs and mallet set. What I do remember is that the yardstick was there, an unspoken tool of discipline. When either parent walked to that doorway and looked up at the yardstick, it meant that I should cease whatever I was doing or saying, NOW!

At the opposite end of the kitchen was a doorway leading to the inside "back porch" between the kitchen and back door. It held the refrigerator and served as a kitchen extension, mud room, and junk depository. At various times such junk included dead and dying plants; new starts of plants (a leaf stuck in a cheese glass of water); a vacuum cleaner; and empty lard pails filled with agates gathered on Whidbey Island. The agates were there for years until the driveway was paved sometime in the late 1950's. Daddy needed rocks to fill in the potholes and figured he'd spent enough time stepping around pails of agates on his way in and out the back door. Mom never got over it. Until sometime during my grade school years, when we had an electric hot water tank installed in the basement, the back porch also held a small hot water tank which the trash burner heated somehow. Before my bath, Mom always ran her hand down the tank to see if there was enough hot water. If not, no bath. In my mind is a scene of Mom and Grandma doing laundry on the back porch, using a borrowed wringer washer. Could they have been washing my diapers?

The first washer I remember for sure was a square, galvanized metal object in the basement. I have the impression it had belonged to Grandma Grimes. When she died Aunt Ruth, Uncle Del and cousin Larry moved in with Grandpa in the next block; perhaps Aunt Ruth brought her own washer. At any rate, Daddy and Uncle Del moved the machine into our basement and in the process dropped it and created a hole the size and shape of a BB in the brown hallway linoleum, where it remained for years until the linoleum was replaced. It always intrigued me. This washer had a wringer which Mom operated by hand, first running the soapy clothes through it into one of the stationary tubs filled with water for rinsing, and then into the other stationary tub for a second rinse, and finally into the clothes basket. Unless it was raining, Mom hung the clothes outside. When it rained, she used the basement clothes lines, which stretched along the ceiling, and she opened the south and north basement windows so the air could circulate through and dry the clothes in a couple of days. Though she had newer washers later on, Mom never had an electric dryer. She claimed she didn't need one, and maybe she was right!

Mom always said that, in addition to myself on more than one occasion, every kid who came into the house fell down the basement stairs. None was hurt seriously. Halfway down the stairs was a screened cupboard called the "pantry." Before my parents had a refrigerator the pantry held butter, milk, pies, and other things which needed to keep cool. In my time, the pantry was used to store boughten canned goods. And just before the pantry, at knee level on the stairs, was the opening to "under the house"--the part which had not been excavated. Often I was sent down to get a can of condensed milk or vegetables, or a jar of home-canned fruit from the fruit cupboard at the bottom of the stairs, and I always had an eerie feeling that something might reach out from the shadows under the house and GRAB me. Actually, the only things under there were kitchen overflow items such as the turkey roasting pan, my potty chair after I outgrew it, and a wash basin, used exclusively for soaking feet (Mom's or Grandma's) and for throwing up (me). The wash basin was light green enamel, and the thought of it still makes me nauseous. Sometimes Butch, the cat, had fits and went into hiding in that dark space or on top of the fruit cupboard, where only his eyes showed.

Besides the washer and stationary tubs, the basement held Daddy's photography lab, his workbench, storage shelves, the coal furnace and the coal bin. Daddy had made his enlarger out of old camera parts, and under the workbench were bottles of chemicals and flat pans for developing black and white photographs. Sometimes I was allowed to watch, sitting out of the way on a high wooden stool. He put a negative in the enlarger, focused the image, and made a test strip--a strip of photo paper which he exposed in small sections for various lengths of time, say for 15, 20, 25, and 30 seconds. Working in the yellow safety light, which wouldn't expose the photo paper, he started by covering all but about an inch of the test strip with another piece of paper. Next, he wound up the counter, another of his inventions made from an old phonograph crank; he had it rigged so it clicked once a second until it wound down. When everything was ready he turned off the safety light,

started the counter, and turned on the enlarger light to expose the paper. He counted to five or ten, then moved the top paper back an inch to expose more of the test strip, and counted five more clicks; he repeated this until all of the test strip was exposed. When he developed it he would know the correct exposure time for the picture.

The coal furnace was installed sometime before I was born. I recall a story about Daddy and Uncle Del or Uncle Roggie going to Seattle with a truck and bringing back their furnaces in pieces, which they then assembled in their basements. The coal bin was in a basement corner, beneath a south window. The coal truck parked in the driveway, and the driver pushed a chute through the open window into the coal bin. Safely standing on the bottom stair step at the other end of the basement, I watched the coal roar down the chute and fill the bin in no time. In the evening before bed Daddy chopped kindling for starting the fire next morning. The formula was: wadded-up newspaper, then kindling, then a little coal on top. While that got going he got dressed and maybe ate some breakfast; then he went back down to shovel in more coal before leaving for work. For the rest of the day it was up to Mom (and to me as I got older) to keep the furnace going by adding a shovelful of coal from time to time. Some people had stokers--small bins attached to the furnace which automatically fed in the coal. Some even had oil furnaces. Auntie Claire and Uncle Roggie were the first of our relatives to get one. I was about eleven when we finally got our oil furnace and a thermostat, which I considered a great status symbol. Until then we could regulate the amount of heat coming from the two registers with a kind of dial located on the wall by the hall register. The dial had levers with chains that ran under the floor and attached to metal disks inside each furnace pipe a couple of feet below each register. By moving the levers a person could partially shut off the air flow from the furnace if it got too hot.

Just off the main floor hall was the bedroom. Before the upstairs was finished, my parents shared their bedroom with me. On one wall were two pictures that glowed in the dark: Walt Disney cartoon characters, Thumper the rabbit and Flower the skunk. Up until I started first grade I slept in a crib and was humiliated when children at my fifth birthday party discovered I was still sleeping in a crib like a baby! One night I dreamed there was a bear under my pillow and an owl roosting on the kitchen stove. When I woke up screaming I knew that under the hot, hard lump in my pillow was a bear. Mom wanted to lift up the pillow to show me there was no bear, but I screamed in terror, knowing the bear would kill us all. Finally I allowed Mom to lift a corner, then more, and finally the whole pillow. The bear dissolved into harmless memory. But that owl was still roosting on the stove, so Mom took my hand and led me to the kitchen, to show me there was no owl.

I was in my crib grieving for a dead puppy when the veterinarian, Dr. Bradbury, came to the house. We only had the little gold and white cocker spaniel for about a week. I wanted to name him Honey, but Daddy convinced me that Sonny was more appropriate for a boy dog, especially once he grew up. Over the weekend we took him on his first

outing, to Whidbey Island, where Daddy took a picture of him in his little harness, standing on the hood of the car. The next morning, however, a big pink swollen glob bulged in the corner of one eye. I cried all the way to the vet, who decided that a grain of sand had irritated the eye. He said he could fix it by lancing it, and that since Sonny was so scared he would use anesthesia so he wouldn't even feel it. So we left him with Dr. Bradbury for the day. Sonny was still asleep when I went with Daddy to pick him up that afternoon, and I sat in the back seat with him, stroking him and telling him how much I loved him, and asking him to wake up. Suddenly, just as we pulled into the driveway, he coughed up some bright red blood, gasped, and lay still. I began to wail, and Mom came running out, looked at Sonny, and took me inside. I wanted to go to bed and crawled into the crib. Mom went to look at Sonny again. When she came back she was crying and said, "I think he's dead."

I stayed in my bed, and after a while Dr. Bradbury came to the house. Later I later learned that he thought the anesthesia had killed Sonny, who had been so scared that he gulped and gulped it. Mom always regretted that she had not stayed with Sonny, thinking that her presence would have soothed him. Before he left, Dr. Bradbury came into the bedroom where I was. He didn't say anything to me, but I heard him say how sorry he was, and he looked at me when he put some money on the dresser. After he left Mom told me it was forty dollars, which was what she had paid for Sonny. I didn't want another dog; I wanted  Sonny. But it wasn't long before we got Rusty, a red Cocker Spaniel with one white spot on his nose. He lived with us for many years.

In that small bedroom my clothes were stored next to the crib in a cardboard "wardrobe" purchased at Montgomery Ward's. After we moved upstairs the wardrobe stood in the upstairs hall and served as an overflow closet. The crib, wardrobe, and my parents' bedroom set (double bed, dresser, chest-of-drawers) all crowded into that small room. Shortly before I began first grade, Daddy purchased an army surplus cot for me to sleep on. Delighted to be rid of the crib, I took to it readily. For years, long after I moved into my own room upstairs with a real bed, that cot went with us on family vacations and saved having to pay for a room (or cabin at an "auto court") with an extra bed for me.

Next to the bedroom, off the main floor hall, was the bathroom with toilet, sink, and tub with shower. Daddy preferred a shower and took one every Saturday night, all his adult life. Mom and I took baths, with Butch-cat perched on a corner of the tub, watching; and between baths we took "spit baths" at the bathroom sink, where, during the week, Daddy washed up every day after work. The bathroom had a medicine cabinet and drawers built into the wall. I can remember sitting on my little potty chair doing my job, while Grandma sat on the toilet doing hers. One morning after breakfast I couldn't produce anything, and Mom told me to sit in my potty chair until I did. Meanwhile she went downstairs to do the wash. Soon I followed her, and when she learned I still hadn't produced she advised me to go back, or I'd be sorry. Very soon I felt a mess in my pants and began to cry in disgust. Perhaps I learned my lesson then, or perhaps later, because Uncle Del claimed that

55

once when I was over at their house I wet my pants, took them off, and carried them home at arm's length.

The remainder of the main floor consisted of the living and dining rooms, with an archway in between. For a long time there was a stout hook in the center of the archway. The hook, I was told, once held my "jumper," a canvas seat on springs, suspended so my feet barely reached the floor, allowing me to jump up and down in safety and exercise vertically before I could walk. I recall none of that, but I do remember my "kiddie-car." This was my stroller with the handle and footrests removed. Sitting astride, I walked myself around the hallway, kitchen, and indoor back porch--at quite a clip, apparently, for I associate this with Mom scowling and the message to slow down and not bash into things.

The living and dining rooms had area rugs on hardwood floors which Daddy had laid, sanded and finished. In the fairly small dining room was the dining table and matching chairs, the china cabinet Daddy had made, and Mom's wind-up Edison phonograph with a storage place for thirty-five Edison records, each a quarter inch thick. They ranged from classical to operatic arias to vaudeville routines, by far the most numerous. Occasionally Mom unloaded the stack of stuff piled on top of the phonograph and allowed me to play the records. Mostly, though, the phonograph sat unused, a relic of "the good old days." We ate in the dining room only when family came for Sunday dinner (usually pot roast or fried chicken) or on holidays. Later, after Grandma broke her hip and came to live with us, we ate the evening meal in the dining room.

The dining room table had many uses besides actual dining. Mom used it for playing solitaire and for laying out patterns and cutting fabric prior to sewing. I used it for homework in high school, and before that, for paper dolls. If Barbie Dolls had been around when I was a child, I'd have been an addict. Baby dolls didn't much interest me. I wanted an adult doll that I could dress up in different outfits, a doll-sized Mrs. Flinnigan that I envisioned as an extension of myself. So I had to settle for paper dolls. Whenever we went downtown I was allowed to pick out a book of paper dolls at Woolworth's or Equals Variety Store. While I favored glamorous women with pages of clothes, I remember Shirley Temple and Margaret O'Brien paper dolls;; and another time I found the Bumstead family: Blondie, Dagwood, Alexander and Cookie.

At home I would set myself up at the dining room table to punch the doll figures out of the stiff paper covers and then cut out their outfits. I persuaded Mom that I'd be extra careful with her sharp kitchen scissors-- which I still have and keep in the desk Daddy got at Monkey Wards. As

56

I cut out the paper dolls' outfits I purposely cut off all the tabs intended to hold the paper clothing on the dolls when they were upright in their stiff cardboard stands. I didn't intend the dolls to be vertical. Instead, I laid them flat on the table and placed their outfits on them, one after the other.

My favorite paper doll of all time had just a few outfits. Instead, she had pages of hair styles of all colors: blonde, brunette, redhead, strawberry blond, etc. There were up-do's pageboys, braids, wavy, curly, straight, bangs, a dip over one eye--every possibility. Each tiny hairdo I cut out very carefully, placing it over the paper doll's bald head and admiring the effect. It kept me busy for hours.

Once the outfits/hairdos were cut out and tried on, most of the fun was over. If the dining room table wasn't needed they stayed there for a few days; then I threw them away and looked forward to the next trip to town.

The door between the hall and living room was always open during the day. I remember hiding behind it once when Grandpa Britt came to deliver eggs. He was married to Roggie's mother and lived on a small farm off the Blodgett Road south of town. Grandpa Britt always wanted to kiss me, and I didn't like his wet, sloppy kisses, so I hoped he would deliver the eggs and leave if he didn't see me. When I hid behind the open door, he thought I was playing hide-and-seek, soon found me, and with great delight planted an especially wet one on my face. Years later I learned that I wasn't the only one he liked to kiss, and that once Mom had told him, "You keep your hands off me!" which made him cry, because he "didn't mean anything."

Both the living and dining rooms had pull-down window shades with fringe and sheer curtains, which Mom washed once or twice a year. She used stretching frames, otherwise stored in the rafters of the garage, to shape and dry the curtains. The frames, which Daddy had made, consisted of thin strips of wood nailed together to form rectangles the exact size of a single curtain. Along each strip, an inch or so apart, were very sharp thin spikes. Mom would push the edges of a damp, washed curtain through the spikes until the curtain was impaled on all edges and stretched tight. She put two or three curtains on each frame and then leaned them against the south side of the house under the kitchen windows. On a warm, sunny day, the only time she washed curtains, they dried in a couple of hours. Then she put them back on their rods and re-hung them, fresh and clean.

Our living room around the time I was born

In my early years the living room held a matching couch and chair, a rocking chair, a radio, and various small pieces such as lamps, end tables and Daddy's smoking stand, an apparatus with a magazine rack below (for the *National Geographic* and *Saturday Evening Post*) and on top small ashtrays and a metal holder for a pack of cigarettes. In our family all the men and none of the women smoked. Lucky Strike was Daddy's brand; Roggie smoked Chesterfields, and Del smoked Camels. The couch and matching chair were dark brown, scratchy to my bare legs, and grossly overstuffed and outdated in my mind. They were second-hand, purchased somewhere in Seattle, perhaps the same place the furnace came from. Aspiring status seeker that I was, I yearned for more modern furniture like the Cannons had across the street, or the Varnadores. The couch and chair were an embarrassment second only to the crib. Finally, when I was in fourth grade, Daddy took a night class in upholstery and transformed the couch and chair into modern-looking furniture.

The radio was a Philco floor-model of polished wood. Its antenna was on a long pole on top of the garage. When everyone wanted to hear a program, such as "The Great Gildersleeve" or "Lux Radio Theater," the radio was turned to a comfortable volume. But if it was something in which only I was interested ("Roy Rogers" or "Jack Armstrong" or "Sergeant Preston of the Yukon") and company was visiting, I turned the volume down and lay on the floor next to the speaker.

Early-on, Daddy added a desk to the living room. I was with him and must have been around four when he bought it at the Montgomery

Ward store downtown, where I saw a child about my age on a leash, just like a dog. In fact, he wore a harness with a strap attached, held by his mother. It seemed to me the ultimate humiliation, worse than having outdated furniture or sleeping in a crib. While I was staring at the dog-child, Daddy bought the desk on the showroom floor. I couldn't believe my eyes when he pointed to a brand new desk of shiny dark wood and said, "In a few days, this will be in our living room." As soon as it was delivered, Daddy told me I could have one of its drawers to store some of my smaller playthings such as half-used crayons, a skate key, blunt scissors, a yo-yo, a jackknife, a watercolor set, or colored pencils. Inevitably, the drawer became a catch-all for whatever clutter I was told to clean up but wasn't ready to discard. Every so often it filled to the brim and I was told, "Janet, it's time to clean out your drawer." Afterwards, just a few important objects rattled around in the bottom.

Daddy used the desk to store records for his floor sanding business and for income tax. After Grandpa died and Daddy became financial secretary for the Carpenters Union, he always went to the desk when carpenters came to pay their dues. But in one of the big drawers at the bottom he stored some black and white photographs, a souvenir book with colored photographs of the 1939 San Francisco World's Fair, and a collection of drawings and paintings he had made while taking a commercial arts correspondence course. I thought the drawings were magnificent, though now I can recall only two, both pencil sketches: one of a half-ruined Greek or Roman temple; the other, wrapped in the blue-prints, our house as he had designed it with no second floor, just an attic. Otherwise, the drawing was totally accurate, including a curved flagstone walk with deodars on either side.

Other living room furniture included a cube-shaped hassock, a round end table with two shelves, and a bookcase Daddy had made. The hassock had a small hole in the top, caused by a dropped cigarette coal. About the time I started to walk I discovered this hole was the perfect size for my finger to explore, as shown in a photograph of me with my finger in the hole and an expression of concentration on my face. The round table, which I still have, was purchased at Northern State Hospital in Sedro-Woolley, produced by occupational therapy patients. The top shelf of the bookcase, which I also still have, was for my collection of glazed pottery ornaments. A succession of songbirds sat there, replacing each other when a head or tail broke off. The one I remember had a top-knot, which Mom thought was especially cute. Bothered by this irregularity, I kept trying to smooth it down. Also on the shelf were "Honey Bear," a bear cub with one paw in a pot of honey; a green pixie sent by Mom's cousin Winifred in California; and a couple of small piggy banks, identical in shape (pig sitting upright with big belly for collecting coins) but different in color and design. One evening when my parents were in the kitchen and there was company in the living room (not relatives this time--probably people from Camera Club or some carpenters and their wives), I passed around my piggy bank and was so delighted with the results I decided to make a second sweep. This time most of the people shook their heads, no, and when Mom came in with coffee the piggy banks went back on the shelf.

At the far end of the living room, the fireplace fascinated me from an early age. Mr. Harris, who lived next door to Grandpa and Auntie Ruth, had built it. The screen stood out from the fireplace and had curved sides to close either end. But the top was open and almost as high as I could reach when I began to walk. It was a perfect place to reach over and drop things. I see myself watching one blue checked slipper and my Teddy bear burst into flame while a parental voice says, "See, this is why I told you not to drop things over the screen." The owner of the voice apparently rescued Teddy, as verified by two color slides: one shows me standing by the round end-table with my first birthday cake; on the floor is a brand new Teddy with a ribbon around his neck. In the other slide I appear to be the same age, but Teddy is considerably worse for wear, charred in several spots.

Next to the fireplace was the upstairs door. Lacking a toy box or bedroom of my own, I stored my toys in a haphazard heap behind the stair door. This seemed perfectly natural until the day Madge Bloom and Ray, who was my age, came over. While Mom and Madge canned peaches in the kitchen, Ray and I were supposed to entertain ourselves playing in the living room. Ray wasn't interested in whatever toys I had out and wanted to see the rest of my toys. When I pointed them out behind the door he was astonished. "Is *that* where you keep your toys?" he squeaked in his high little voice. I mentally added "toy storage" to "crib" and "couch & chair" on my List of Personal Embarrassments.

60

My favorite toy of all time, my doll house, was too big to fit behind the upstairs door. It was a cheap affair made of shiny cardboard with painted walls and windows. Gradually I accumulated furniture for the six rooms: a kitchen, dining room and living room on the ground floor; and a bath separating two bedrooms on the second floor. Now on trips

downtown I had to decide between a book of paper dolls or a piece of furniture for the doll house. All the furniture was plastic, and so were the people. The man, who wore a suit and tie, and woman, wearing a pink dress, had joints at the shoulders, knees and hips, so they could sit or stand. The baby, about the size of a pea, lay in a crib in the nursery. I liked to dump everything out so the rooms were bare, then gradually furnish the house. While I tried different arrangements, the furniture always seemed to end up the same way, even in the kitchen.

While I don't remember falling down the basement stairs, the stairway to the second floor is a different matter. I recall two incidents. The first time, I was probably three or four and don't remember the tumble itself so much as the aftermath. Grandma was babysitting, and she soothed my bumps and bruises in the big rocking chair in the living room. I had about finished bawling when someone came in the back door, and as soon as I realized it was Daddy I commenced again at full volume and succeeded in getting another round of comfort. The second tumble occurred when I was a bit older, dressed up as "Mrs. Flinnigan." I had on Mom's old clothes and Auntie Claire's high heels (her small shoes were a better fit that Mom's) and paused at the top of the stairs, preparing for a sweeping descent. Instead, my high heels got tangled on the top step. I recall thinking, "Oh-oh, I'm going to fall down the stairs" before plunging to the bottom in a distinctly unglamorous manner. To my knowledge, the last person to fall down those stairs was my college roommate, Janet Bay. She came home with me for the weekend and made quite an impression. The worst damage was to her sense of dignity.

A further word about Mrs. Flinnigan, my grown-up, glamorous persona, who did everything in excess. She dripped luxurious clothing (mainly purple, my favorite color), priceless jewelry and sophistication. She had big breasts, which I called "fat ribs," lived in a huge house with a swimming pool, drove the latest and biggest Cadillac (a cardboard box on the living room floor) and smoked (a rolled-up piece of paper secured with scotch tape and darkened with a pencil at one end to resemble ashes) constantly. Mrs. Flinnigan was the consummate snob, given to high falutin' pretensions, a cross between my playmate Lonnie Varnadore's pretty young mother, a paper doll, and a department store manikin, which is what I wished my mother looked like.

Mrs. Flinnigan paraded around in Mom's and Auntie Claire's castoff clothes, scarves, hats, and shoes. When she got sick she had all the diseases I had heard of all at once: flu, mumps, measles, scarlet fever, polio, whooping cough and an abscessed tooth. When she went out she flung a fur stole ("Patsy") around her neck and stuck her nose high in the air.

Mrs. Flinnigan's fur was actually a long dead, moth eaten marten with a metal clip in its mouth, a gift to me from Julia, a friend of Mom's. Probably Patsy still had some fur when I first got her, but I remember her only as a long strip of soft suede, with black eyes and nose and the clip, used for fastening her head to her tail when she was a fashionable neck piece. When Mrs. Flinnigan wasn't wearing Patsy around her neck I carried her around and stroked away all her fur. After I grew old enough to give up Patsy I wondered at the fashion of bygone days, when a woman would fling that sad, worn-out thing around her neck. Here's a poem I wrote as an adult:

She swirled about in velvet and chiffon,
chin thrust high, eyes, derisively downcast.
Donning purple when she could find it, she
flung fox fur about her neck before stepping out
in high, high heels that clicked importantly.
Bejeweled horn-rims rested halfway down her nose--
when not swept off in a flourish.
A master of artistic smoking, she allowed
a thick cloud to ooze from parted lips before

62

sucking deep and exhaling with studied nonchalance.
Her rule of thumb: excess in everything.
Ailments, for instance. She had flu, polio, pneumonia,
scarlet fever, measles and chicken pox
--simultaneously.

I try to see her:
an old rayon dress hitched up at the waist,
some kind of moth-eaten weasel at the neck,
heels, dragging, catching, flopping off,
bent sunglasses with the lenses knocked out;
a rolled-up strip of paper precisely the right length,
secured by Scotch tape, held adroitly between
index and middle fingers,
at intervals brought to the lips for a drag.

I wish someone had thought to take my picture.

Before the upstairs was finished its walls were plasterboard (similar to drywall), and the floor consisted of rough, wide boards. The stairwell had no protective railing, so I had to be careful not to get too close to the edge. The stairs came up into the hallway, and off the hallway were two future bedrooms and the attic. Between the bedrooms was a future bathroom with plumbing for a sink and toilet. There were two openings to the attic, one from the hall and another from the smaller bedroom, which would be mine. One of the floorboards in my room had a knothole bigger than my fist, and I was uneasy to go near it, being so close to the dark, dusty attic. Sometimes at night I dreamed that big green snakes came out of the hole, slithered downstairs where I thought I was safe, crawled up my legs and GOT me! It was a relief when Daddy eventually laid a hardwood floor and covered that hole once and for all.

Until the upstairs was finished the only furniture there were Mom's treadle sewing machine and Daddy's reed organ, which he had built from cast-off pieces of pianos and I'm not sure what else. It sat in the hall next to the stairwell, and often in the evening, especially in winter, he went up to play it. Sometimes I sat on his lap, cozy and warm, while he pumped the pedals and worked the two keyboards, playing "Wedding of the Winds," "The Skaters' Waltz," and other favorites. There was no heat upstairs, ever, except for what rose up from the lower hall into my bedroom through a register Daddy cut in the floor.

When I was in first grade, in the spring, the upstairs was finished.

First the plasterers came. By the time I got home from school they were finishing up, and I was furious to learn that Lonnie Varnadore, who went to kindergarten in the morning only, was upstairs watching them work. No fair!--it wasn't even his house! Next, Daddy laid the hardwood floor in the bedrooms and hallway, then sanded and varnished it. In the hall he built a protective railing around the stairwell, and he moved the organ into the attic next to my room. He installed woodwork around the windows and doorframes and hung doors from each bedroom to the bathroom. The bedroom doors to the hallway came later, when we could afford them. He finished the closet in the big bedroom and built storage drawers under the eaves. Mom moved the bed linens from the downstairs closet into these drawers along with her dress patterns and cloth scraps.

The bathroom had green linoleum tiles on the floor. Though I had missed out on the plastering, I got to watch the Purvis brothers install the sink and toilet. Above the sink Daddy hung a mirror with a rough spot in one corner where a calendar had been attached. On one side of the mirror was a glamorous woman holding a lighted candle and wearing a see-through negligee--and nothing else! The mirror hung there for over thirty years, until the house was sold.

my first storybook doll

In my room, Daddy made a door to shut off the attic, and he made me a closet under the eaves. Besides holding my clothes, it became the storage place for toys and items I wasn't quite ready to throw away, such as the plaster cast from my broken ankle, old ballet costumes, headless dolls, and similar debris. Every so often Mom ordered me to clean out my closet. Above the closet doors was a little horizontal wedge of space perfect for displaying my growing collection of storybook dolls. Daddy made a glass door, hinged at the top, to protect the dolls from dust. My only furniture at first was a double bed (spool design, borrowed from--I think--Aunt Ruth), a chest of drawers, and a small cedar chest. All the walls upstairs were white until I was in high school and had to have a "home project" for the required home economics course. My project was to redecorate my room, which I painted "sea green" over the summer. A new double bed with box springs and mattress and an up-to-date headboard with sliding panels and

64

space to store things replaced the spool bed. New drapes and a bright pink quilted bedspread completed the project.

My windows faced south. Directly below was the double driveway, shared with the house next door, and two houses away tall poplar trees rose above the rooftops. On clear nights the moon played hide and seek among the branches. Lying in bed, I could hear the peacocks, screaming in their pen at Hillcrest Park two long blocks away, and the train whistle from south of town. These sounds, and even the wind on stormy nights, when its full force hit the side of the house, were my lullaby, easing me to sleep.

The backyard, with Mom and Dad standing beside the garage

Original floor plan of house with half-basement and no second floor. Main floor mostly accurate as to actual construction

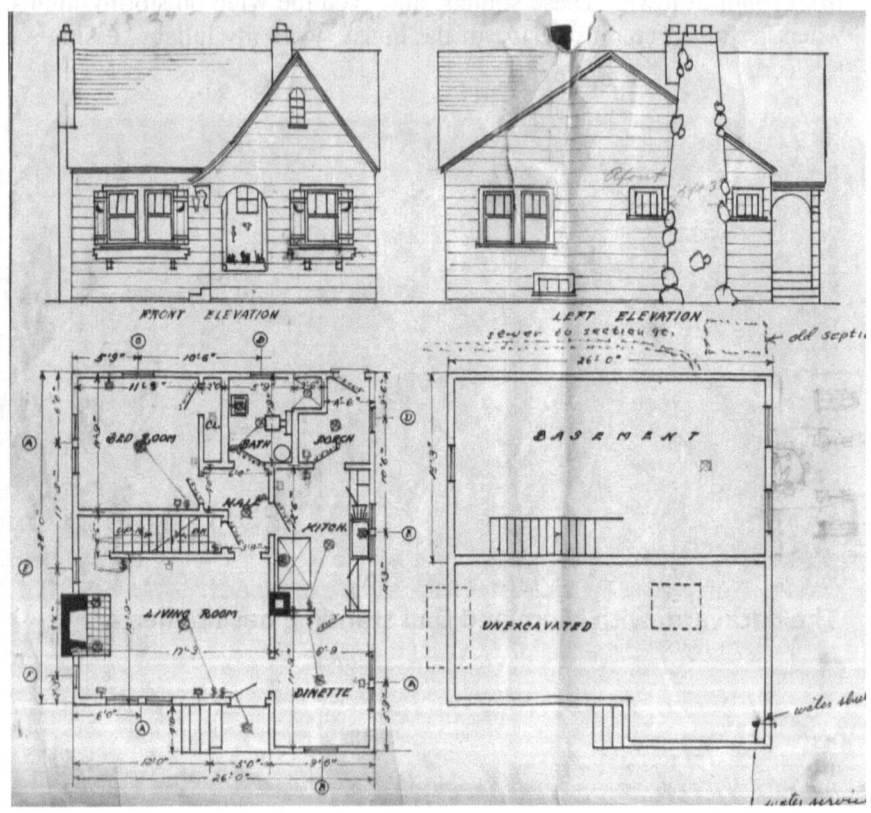

THE NEIGHBORHOOD

Beyond the house, my world expanded as I grew. Long after my parents died and the house was sold, Aunt Ruth still lived just a half block from where I grew up. I visited her there regularly until well into my sixties, and together we would walk around the old neighborhood. Almost every house I passed stirred memories that otherwise might have rested undisturbed and forgotten.

Our house was on Lincoln Hill at the corner of South Eleventh and Section Streets. Eleventh Street ends two long blocks south of there at Hillcrest Park--one neighborhood boundary in my early years. Follow Eleventh Street two short blocks north of our house, past Aunt Ruth's house and Lincoln School, to Broad Street. Across Broad Street from the school was the "little store"--another boundary. West of our house, Tenth Street was the last street on that part of the hill and the third boundary. Beyond Tenth the land dropped sharply to the Skagit flats, site of more residences, the railroad tracks, Highway 99, the business district, the Skagit River, more businesses and houses on the West Side, and then farmland all the way to La Conner and what was then called the Swinomish Slough. The fourth boundary of my neighborhood was Thirteenth street--the easternmost residential street until after the War. Everything east of Thirteenth, like everything beyond the West Side, was "out in the country."

BICYCLE

Most of the time I moved around the neighborhood on foot, though I did have other means of transportation. When I was the right age I got a brand new tricycle, which I remember picking out in the store. It was dark red with white accents and was fairly big, because I rode it until I was about six years old, up the sidewalk to Twelfth Street and down to Hazel Street at the south end of our block.

When I outgrew it I wanted a bicycle. Training wheels hadn't been invented, but there were small bicycles, only slightly bigger than my tricycle, and I wanted one of those. If I fell off I would be pretty close to the ground. But my parents couldn't afford something I would outgrow in just a year or two, nor could they afford a full-size brand new bike. However, Mom's old bicycle, which she hadn't used for several years, was in the garage. Daddy agreed to let me try riding it, but it was impossible because my legs weren't long enough to reach the pedals, even with the seat in its lowest position. That was solved by removing the seat altogether, which left the shaft sticking straight up, threatening to impale me. But how likely was that? Nobody wore helmets then, just as cars didn't have seat belts. It was hard to balance without a seat to sit on, but I was determined. I had to start out pumping right away and wobbled down the sidewalk with Daddy running behind, holding onto the back fender to keep me steady. After several days of this Daddy began letting go when I picked up speed, and bye and bye I could ride on my own--but always on the sidewalk, never in the street--at least not within sight of the house.

As soon as I could ride the bike I gave my tricycle to Lonnie Varnadore, which made Mom mad. She felt his family could afford to buy him a tricycle. Perhaps she had some more needy child in mind, or planned to sell it.

So I had a bicycle, but it embarrassed me. Once I grew enough to sit on the seat, there was still the problem of the stand. New bikes had kick stands, but Mom's old bike's stand, a U-shaped device, was attached to either side of the rear wheel's hub and, when not in use, to the bottom of the back fender with a clip. To use the stand you released the clip and pulled down the stand to lift the rear wheel off the ground and brace the bike upright. I hated it, it was so out-of-date. Why bother taking care of the bike? I was supposed to keep it in the garage but usually just flung it down in the side yard under the kitchen windows, where it rusted in the rain. I refused to use the stand.

Mom's bicycle, eventually mine

68

At some point I started saving my allowance for a new bike. I still have an old West Coast Telephone Company envelope with a note from Aunt Claire, "for your new bike," referring to money enclosed. The savings accumulated slowly, however, and eventually I decided to use the money to spiff up the old bike. With Daddy's help, I sanded away the rust and painted the bike with shiny blue enamel. I got a new seat, painted the handle bars metallic silver, and bought new black rubber grips for the handles. Best of all, we replaced the hideous rear-wheel stand and its clip with a kick stand. All that remained of the old stand was a small hole at the bottom of the rear fender where the clip had been attached. The final touch was a new wire basket in front of the handlebars.

I wasn't exactly proud of my refurbished bike, but at least it no longer embarrassed me, and after that I did store it in the garage, at least most of the time. Even so, I never rode it very far--just around the neighborhood and down to the park.

OUR BLOCK

My pre-school world focused on two blocks: "our" block and Auntie Ruth's block just north of ours, across Section Street. By the time I was ten I had been inside most of the houses in those two blocks.

At first, Uncle Ed and Nina Jacobs lived just south of us on Eleventh Street in a tiny little house far back from the street, near the alley. It had just two rooms--a living room/kitchen and a bedroom, plus a bathroom, and a big lawn from the house to the street. When I was born their son, Jimmy, was about twelve, and the only thing I remember about him from that time was when he came over to tell us that he had joined

Jimmy Jacobs

the Navy right after the end of the War. He made a career in the Navy and rose to the rank of Commander before being shot down in 1967, during the Vietnam War. His remains were never found. Twice I've touched his name on the Vietnam Memorial in Washington, D.C.

69

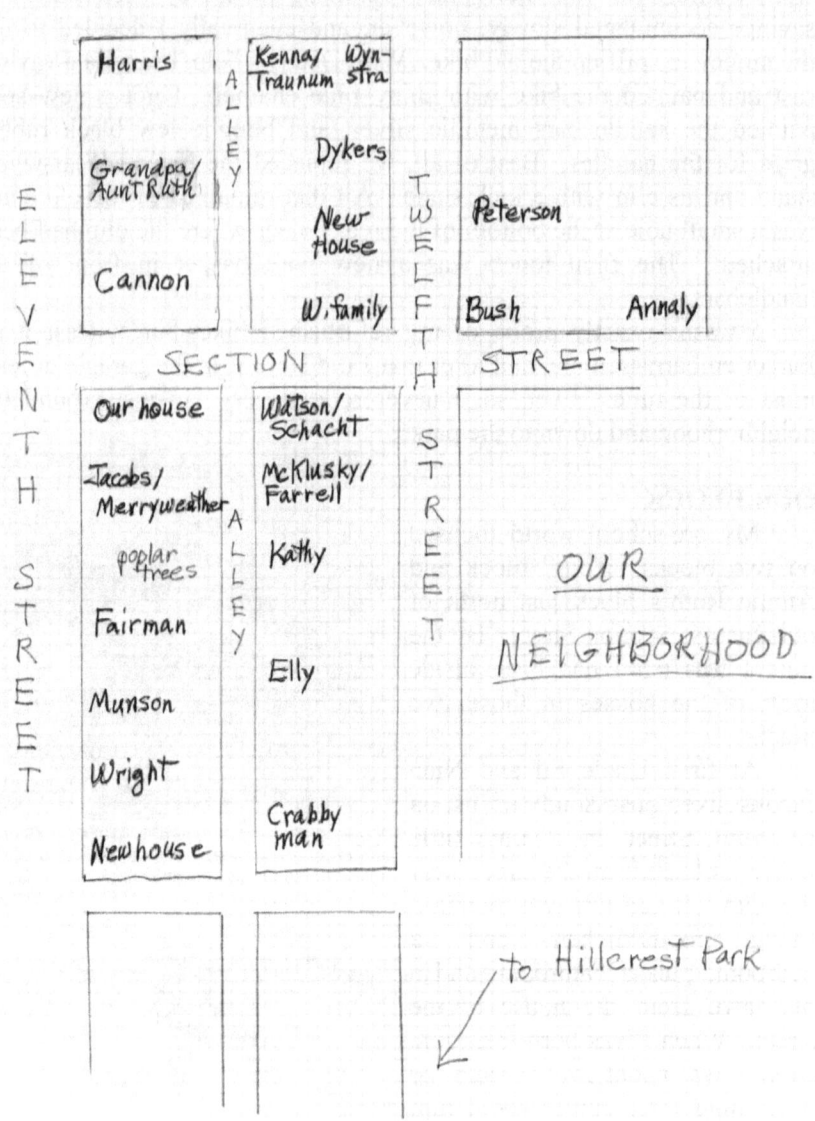

ELEVENTH STREET

Harris

ALLEY

Kenna/ Traunum

Wyn-stra

Grandpa/ Aunt Ruth

Dykers

New House

Cannon

W. family

SECTION STREET

TWELFTH STREET

Peterson

Bush Annaly

Our house

Watson/ Schacht

Jacobs/ Merryweather

McKlusky/ Farrell

ALLEY

poplar trees

Kathy

STREET

Fairman

Elly

OUR

NEIGHBORHOOD

Munson

Wright

Crabby man

Newhouse

to Hillcrest Park

70

When Ed and Nina moved to their new house on the West Side we got new neighbors. One night I was down in our basement with Daddy, watching him develop wedding pictures of some people I didn't know named Dick and Esther. Dick Merryweather was Nina's half-brother, and soon they moved into the little house next door. Dick had one blue eye and one brown eye, and a tattoo on his arm which he had gotten in the Marines. Esther was fun to visit. She told me years later that I would come in, announce that I could stay five minutes, and then spend those five minutes asking how much time was left before I had to go home. Dick built a new house on the big lawn in front of the little house while he and Esther (and eventually baby Gloria) were still living in the little house. By the time I finished first grade the foundation and floor were laid. I remember playing with Lonnie, jumping off the foundation with a cast on my left leg, having broken my ankle while trying to jump rope and cross the street at the same time. My first babysitting job was with Gloria. Esther had to go somewhere, and Dick was working inside the new house, which by then was framed and sided. My job was to stay in the little house with Gloria, who was sleeping, and to go get Dick if she woke up and began to cry.

Mom always warned me not to make a pest of myself when "visiting" (hence the five minute limit); nevertheless, shortly after the Merryweathers moved into the new house a terrible thing happened. Gloria, who had recently begun walking, had a little rattle that I especially liked. On the bottom was a round suction cup which I liked to stick on the floor or the wall and bat the rattle around. I had just stuck it against the blue kitchen wall when Mom called for me to come home for supper. Having been taught to put things back where I found them, I pulled the rattle off the wall, and with it came a circle of blue paint just the size of the suction cup, exposing the white plaster beneath. I was horrified and burst into tears, convinced I had ruined the Merryweathers' new house. Esther tried to comfort me, but Gloria immediately toddled over to the white circle and began picking at it, so that Esther had to move the highchair in front of it to keep her hands out of range. Before long Dick repaired the damage, and Esther made a special point of showing me how you couldn't even see where the white circle had been.

The Merryweathers' welcome mat was always out. One time when I was visiting, Esther told me she was going to have another baby--who turned out to be a second daughter, Ann. When they got television, long before we did, I was invited (no doubt after some artless hinting) to watch some favorite shows. The Merryweathers were wonderful neighbors and lived there until they died. I always visited them when I went home.

71

Over the years several families lived in the house next to the Merryweathers. Their yard had the poplar trees I could see from my bedroom window. In the house beyond that Judy Fairman lived during my pre-school days. She was a year older than I, and we used to play with Michael Monson, who was even older and lived in the house beyond Judy's. I didn't like playing with them very much; Mom said they ganged up on me. Judy may have had good reason. I was told that my first--and perhaps only--spanking occurred when Judy and I were playing on our living room floor with my pegs and mallet set, taking turns pounding the colored wooden pegs through the board. Suddenly I bonked Judy instead of a peg. Another time we were playing house on Judy's red cement front steps. I was supposed to lie down on one of the steps, like a bed, and cover myself with a gunny sack. I didn't want to, because the gunny sack had a big wet spot. But Judy made me do it anyway, and then she and Michael picked on me until I ran screaming home, with them in hot pursuit. As I crossed Ed and Nina's big front lawn Mom came out the back door and yelled at them to leave me alone. I went inside and helped Mom and Grandma, who were preparing corn for canning, cutting the kernels off the cobs in long, flat swaths.

An older couple, the Wrights, lived in the house beyond the Monsons. Many years later I learned that their grandson was Larry Stevens, who became president of Tacoma Community College during part of my career there. They had a little shallow fish pond in a grove of trees near the sidewalk. One summer day something happened that for a long time made me afraid even to walk past the Wright's pond. A little boy somehow almost drowned in that shallow water. After that, I could never go near that pond without feeling that something like Grandma's boogeyman was about to grab my leg and drag me in.

Beyond the Wright's house was a vacant lot at the corner of Hazel Street, the end of the block. One day Daddy said, "Come on, let's walk down the street; there's something going on." We walked to the end of the block (I wasn't afraid to pass Wright's fish pond with Daddy), and in the vacant lot was a big yellow machine digging a huge hole. Daddy said it was making a basement for a house. Before long the house was finished--temporarily. It was very small--a white square box with a smaller box attached at one end. The big box was the living room and kitchen and the little box was the bedroom. The Wilders moved in with their boy Bruce, several years older than I and too big to play with. Daddy said that eventually the Wilders planned to build more, but it was many years before they did and then another family, the Matthesons, bought the house.

72

The house across the alley from us faced Twelfth Street and belonged to the Watsons. Their boy, Eddie, was also too old for me to play with. Eddie had a dog, Fella, who barked all night, though I slept through it. Later they moved to another house in the same block but farther south on Twelfth Street. Then Mr. and Mrs. Schacht, an older couple, moved in. Mrs. Schacht was always pleasant and bought Campfire Girl mints from me every year. One time Mom cracked up when she read my list of customers, including "Mrs. Shot."

When I was born, the McCluskys lived next to the Watsons, across the alley from Ed and Nina. Mr. McClusky worked for the State Patrol, and played an important role in my birth, as shown in a newspaper clipping. The McCluskys had a big girl, Suzanne, who walked through our alley on her way to Lincoln School. She was nice to me but was too old to play with. Her brothers were Billy, a year older than me, and Bobby, a year younger. Billy's nose ran a lot, and he tended to wipe his upper lip with his tongue; I was a little afraid of him, especially after I wore my old winter coat outside and announced that it was now my play coat, and Billy asked, "Does that mean I can throw dirt on it?" I remember standing safely on our back porch, shouting to Billy in the alley, "You're a nasty Jap!" and Billy shouting back, "Yeah-yeah, you're a dirty Hitler!" Eventually the McCluskys had a baby sister, Dinah. Mrs. McClusky was in the back yard shelling peas, watching Dinah in her play pen, and I was walking around their yard in my bare feet when I stepped on a bee. Mrs. McClusky carried me home howling. I was proud to have achieved the milestone of my first bee sting, but I hadn't realized how much it would hurt.

WINS RACE WITH STORK

Dr. Harold Madsen of this city won a race with the stork last evening but sharing in his victory today is State Patrolman William McClusky.

Dr. Madsen was on a case near an English logging camp when the Mount Vernon General hospital tried to locate him for Mrs. Forrest Grimes of this city. Since there was no telephone where the doctor was, the aid of the state patrol was enlisted. Officer McClusky drove to the camp to tell him of the stork's impending visit, then acted as his escort to the hospital.

A few moments after Dr. Madsen arrived, Mrs. Grimes gave birth to a 7 pound, 4 ounce daughter. Both mother and daughter are getting along nicely, attendants said today.

73

The McCluskys moved to Conway long before I started school, and the B. family moved into their house. Bobby B. was a year older than I; his brother Mark was a year or two younger. They were nice boys. I remember mainly playing in their backyard on their swing set--the nicest one I ever saw. After we had played for a while, Mrs. B. would call us inside for cookies and milk or sometimes apple juice. I had not had apple juice before and thought it was wonderful. One day Mom told me Mrs. B. was going to have a baby and warned me not to stare or ask questions. I knew babies grew inside a woman, but I hadn't realized it would change her shape, and day after day I watched Mrs. B's belly get bigger. One day I came home from playing with Bobby and Mark and said in disgust, "Boy, Mrs. B. is just getting so fat!" Mom replied, "Why, that's her little baby!" Oh! It finally got through my thick head.

They named the baby Robin, and by the time she was born the B's had moved to the Monson house, down Eleventh Street from us. They lived there just a short time before they had to leave town and move to back East to live with relatives. Mr. B., who looked just like Bobby only bigger and wore a hat, had done something he shouldn't have with some money from the Baptist Church, where he was a deacon and sang in the choir, and where I went to Sunday school with Bobby and Mark. They sold all their furniture, and Esther and Dick Merryweather bought their bedroom set.

AUNTIE RUTH'S BLOCK

Across Section Street from us was Auntie Ruth's block, with just three houses along Eleventh Street. The Cannons lived in the first house. They were an older couple, with three grown children. Their son, Bud, was in the war flying planes, and later in a German prison camp. Their daughters, Anita and Betty, were both married, and for a while Anita, her husband, Lon Varnadore, and my playmate Lonnie lived at the Cannon's. Lonnie was almost two years younger than I and was another nice playmate, meaning he didn't pick on me. Instead, I picked on him. Since I was bigger, I could and did beat him up. I would grab his hair with my left hand and pound the top of his head as hard as I could with my right. Daddy once told me, in no uncertain terms, that I was not to kick Lonnie in the shins any more. I didn't know what shins were, so Daddy explained. Next time I got mad at Lonnie I made sure to kick him in the shins until he fell down screaming.

Often, though, Lonnie and I played together amicably. We would run the length of Cannons' wide front porch and sail off the end shouting, "Bombs away!" And we went into the bushes, took down our pants, and peed. Lonnie could make his pee come out in a nice arc, but mine just ran straight down, sometimes into my shoe. Because of Lonnie I discovered that the difference between boys and girls was more than the the length of their hair and the clothes they wore. Before that I wondered how, when a baby was born, you could tell whether it was a boy or girl, since all babies had short hair or none at all.

The Cannons had a big house filled with all sorts of bric-a-brac. Mrs. Cannon was into ceramics. Everywhere were things which I had to be careful not to touch or bump into. Sometimes my hands seemed to want to reach out and grab something breakable and throw it, as much to break the tension as the object. If Mom had ever been in the Cannons' house she probably would have placed it off limits. All her life she recalled how, while shopping in Vancouver, BC, I bumped into a display table of china and crystal, causing every item to quiver. Maybe she thought she would have to pay for anything I broke, or perhaps we would all be imprisoned and never return to our own country. But Mom was never invited inside the Cannon's house. They and their daughters had their own set of friends. In retrospect, the ones I recall were probably friends of Anita and her sister Betty, rather than of Mrs. Cannon. The women I remember were young and pretty, like Anita and Betty. They all wore dark lipstick and smoked. Lonnie and I would sit in the dining room watching these women talk and blow smoke and make smoke rings. One woman was especially impressive. She dragged on her cigarette then opened her mouth and let the smoke start to float out like a big white cloud before sucking it in and blowing it out in the regular way. It was all very glamorous to me. I wanted to smoke and wear high heels and fur neckpieces and beautiful clothes like Anita and Betty and their friends--so I created Mrs. Flinnigan.

One day Lonnie and I discovered a row of empty milk bottles in the Cannons' garage. The milkman delivered milk regularly, leaving full bottles on the front porch early in the morning and picking up the empty bottles, which had been washed and put out the night before. The milk was pasteurized, but not homogenized until I was older, and the cream rose to the top of the bottle. It could be scooped off carefully and used in coffee or for cooking. Or the bottle could be shaken to mix the skim milk and cream, like the whole milk we buy today. When Lonnie and I discovered the empty milk bottles, his Uncle Bud, now home from the War, was babysitting. But he was sick with mumps which he had gotten from Lonnie, and we knew he couldn't come outside. How we got started I don't know, but all of a sudden Lonnie and I were throwing those milk bottles against the concrete wall at the back of the garage, one at a time, shivering in delight at the sound of breaking glass. Every time a bottle hit the wall I thought of that bric-a-brac in the Cannons' house;

then I threw another one. Bud pounded on the window. He moved his mouth and shook his fist. Lonnie and I looked at him and at each other, and then we threw more bottles. We broke every one of them. Later Bud called my parents, and then he wanted to talk to me. He told me how he was going to have to clean up all that glass once he got well. He hoped I was sorry, but I wasn't sorry, I was afraid--not of what my parents might do, but of Bud. He had been in the War. Maybe he had killed a German. Maybe he would kill me. I was glad when my punishment turned out to be nothing more than a scolding, well worth enduring for the pleasure of breaking all that glass.

North of the Cannons, the middle house in the block belonged to Grandpa Grimes until he died when I was in second grade. This house was where Grandpa's family had lived when they first came to Mount Vernon in 1919 after the First World War. A photograph shows Jim and Clara Grimes and their four children standing in front of the house. Forrest (Daddy), Carol and Ruth appear to have reached adult height; Howard is shorter--perhaps about ten years old. The house has a covered front porch with supporting posts running across the front. Daddy lived there until he and Mom got married. By the time of my earliest memories, Auntie Ruth, Grandpa, Uncle Del, and my cousin Larry were living there. The house had been completely remodeled during the Depression. The big front porch was gone, and a basement had been dug under the house while the family was living above.

There was a big yard. When I was quite small a grape arbor stood on the south side, with a picket fence and two seats facing each other made of white slats like the fence. The grape leaves and curling tendrils made a shady place to sit on a hot day. On the north side of the house was a cherry tree, so much a part of my childhood that I wrote an essay about it:

Aunt Ruth's Cherry Tree

"A tree contains more information than all the libraries in the world," writes E.M. Schumacher in *Small is Beautiful*. Aunt Ruth's cherry tree was a major source of knowledge for me between the ages of nine and twelve. I knew it intimately. My cousin Kay, six years younger, had a swing in the tree, and sometimes, when I had nothing better to do, I pushed her in it. I learned to shinny up one of the ropes. But a swing is a ground thing. You get to know a tree by being in it, by climbing. Aunt Ruth's cherry tree was where I learned to climb.

I remember parts of that tree as sharply as I remember Grandma's face. Where the trunk forked, about level with the top of my head, a thick branch jutted out eight or ten inches to form a kind of saddle before curving upward. I would grab that branch, hook my foot under a knot for an anchor, and hoist myself up until I straddled the branch. As I grew taller and became more accustomed to this process, I refined it to a single flowing motion: grab, hook, hoist—I was up. Over the years, I polished that saddle smooth.

Once up, I had several choices. About five feet higher than the saddle and to one side was a short branch which grew perpendicular to the trunk. It stuck out in such a way that it was a clear drop to the ground, some ten feet below. Its purpose was obvious.

Aunt Ruth and Cherry Tree; Lincoln School at left

Holding the main trunk with my right hand, I could grab the branch, first with my left hand, then with my right. Next I let go with my feet, swung out and dangled. When satisfied, I dropped. Once or twice I dared to hang by my knees for a few seconds, but mostly I dangled and dropped.

Sometimes my friends Sharon and Nancy climbed with me. I recall an incident when Sharon and I were dangling and dropping from that branch, but Nancy was afraid to let go. Though Sharon and I bullied her, she would not drop. Merciless, I threatened to get a pin from Aunt Ruth and jab her; I even went inside pretending to get it. Little Kay was so impressed she still remembers. Nancy screamed and cried, but she would not drop and eventually had to climb down by way of the saddle. After that, I had little respect for her. She was a scaredy-cat.

Closer to the ground, slightly higher than the saddle,

77

another branch about five inches in diameter grew horizontally for five or six feet toward the sidewalk and then forked. I could walk on this branch out to the fork by holding onto smaller branches above, or I could straddle the branch and boost myself along. The fork provided a comfortable seat, where someone like Nancy might read a book. I preferred to work up a bouncing rhythm, pretending the branch was a galloping horse and the trembling leaves a dangerous forest through which I rode, pursued by wild beasts. Tired of this, I might secure one branch of the fork behind my knees, hook my feet under the other branch, and swing over backward to hang with arms dangling toward the grass. Or I could somersault between the fork's branches and end up hanging by my hands, bare toes brushing the ground.

Studying the tree, I studied the seasons. After a winter's absence I approached it as an old friend, ready to renew acquaintance and get on with things. Standing in a comfortable fork, I pondered the corrugated twigs, smaller than my little finger. As the days passed, reddish-brown buds, clustered at the end of each twig, began to swell. Somehow I always missed the first blossom. The buds seemed to burst overnight, covering the tree with white blossoms, inviting to bees. Studying them in detail as they crawled among the petals, I observed grains of pollen on their furry backs and noted the colored lumps of pollen baskets on their legs.

Almost as suddenly as the blossoms had arrived, they were gone, leaving the tree seemingly unchanged except for the carpet of white petals beneath. Soon, though, leaves began to emerge, and I noticed tiny green swellings at the ends of little stems. First they were the size of match heads, then the size of my thumbnail, and finally full-sized, ripe, red-and-yellow cherries. Sitting on a high branch, eating cherries and spitting the pits as far as possible. I was content. After the cherries were gone, on occasion I plucked a leaf, shredded it, and contemplated the network of veins. A cherry leaf has two outer layers, which peel apart in small patches to reveal the veins.

As winter approached, in my idleness I more closely examined the bare tree's bark. In places it was thin, where climbing had polished away its natural roughness. I found I could peel off thin strips of polished bark in long tendrils, which I used to make thick bark braids, imagining I was a jungle girl, surviving like Tarzan, using my wits and the natural materials around me.

Climbing as high as possible in the tree provided my greatest challenge. Gradually I learned the best foot and hand holds as I extended my explorations. A day came in late fall, when most of the leaves were gone, that I reached the highest secure handhold. It was strong enough to stand on, if only there were something above for my hands. However, above were only spindly branches and twigs, which would not bear my weight, though they might help with balance. Carefully, I slid my hand a few inches along the branch, placed one foot where the hand had been, and shifted my weight to that foot. Moving only my head, I checked above to be sure there was space to stand up. Then, spine rigid, I slowly straightened the leg holding my weight. Below and all around me was the tree. Only my eyes moved. After several seconds, I slowly let myself down until my hands touched a firm branch. I sighed, took a deep breath, and screamed my loudest, most blood-curdling Tarzan cry.

Perhaps I climbed to the very top again, but not often. Repeatedly risking myself held no appeal. I had proven I could do it and was satisfied. It did not occur to me then that I was no different from Nancy in my fear—just more fortunate in that no one witnessed it.

In the tree I studied nature and the seasons, tested my skills, and encountered my limitations. The tree, too, had limitations. Eventually Uncle Del paved the adjacent driveway, and during the preparation of the roadbed he cut through a large root. Soon the tree withered and died. Much later I learned why it was cut down, for when that happened I had long since stopped climbing trees. Perhaps by then I had left home, for I did not note the tree's passing. At some forgotten point it became a memory.

At the corner of Eleventh and Section Streets, north of Auntie Ruth's house, was the Harris place. It looked like Auntie Ruth's house in the picture from long ago, with a big covered porch all across the front. Mr. and Mrs. Harris' children were grown up. One of their granddaughters, Ellen, was just two days older than I; we and our mothers had been in the hospital together. The Harris yard was overgrown, and the house was gray for want of paint; it was too much for them now. Mrs. Harris was very sweet and smiling whenever I walked past. They had a dog, Blackie, whom Mr. Harris loved. When Blackie died they buried him in the backyard, and Mr. Harris had a tombstone

("Blackie Harris") made for him, just like at the cemetery.

Kitty corner from the Harris house was Lincoln School, which I attended for eight years. But at first I had to stay in Auntie Ruth's block except when I was sent to "the little store" just beyond the school. This was after I could be trusted to look both ways before crossing the street. Mom would make out a list and give me some money, and the storekeeper, Mr. Nicholas, would get the things on the list, put them in a sack, and give me the change. I was a little bit afraid of him, because I had heard that he was crabby with kids. Mom typically was part way into a recipe when she discovered she lacked some essential ingredient. When I was nine or ten she sent me to the store three times for the same recipe. After that I always asked her to read the recipe through and to check the cupboards before I went to the store. Sometimes in the summer Mom and Auntie Ruth and I walked to the store to get ice cream cones. There were just three flavors: vanilla, strawberry and chocolate. Even while holding Mom's hand, I practiced concentrating on looking both ways while crossing the street on the way back home. More than once, when safely across, I held up my cone to take a lick and the ice cream was gone. There it was, in the middle of the street we had just crossed. Crossing the street and holding the cone upright at the same time were more than I could handle. Later on the store offered dixie cups, ice cream bars and popsicles. My favorite flavors were root beer and banana.

But mostly I stayed on Auntie Ruth's block. At Harris' corner I could turn right and walk up Skagit Street, crossing the alley, to a house facing north, where Joey Kenna lived, and later the Traunum family. Joey was the nicest little boy I ever knew and grew up to be a priest. Even when I accidentally hit him in the head with the business end of a hoe (I was whirling it in a circle and he walked into it) and he ran home howling, he came back later with a little bottle of milk and some animal crackers to share and show me that he wasn't mad. Joey had two sisters in high school, Joanne and Carolyn, who wore jangly charm bracelets, and two grandmothers who were deaf and dumb. Mrs. Kenna and the grandmothers talked to each other with their hands. Joey could understand a little of what they said. His father, Mr. Kenna, had heart trouble.

Joey and I played "doctor" and "house," but nothing naughty happened like peeing outside with Lonnie, even though Joey was a year older than I. When we played house we called each other Pa and Ma. One time, in the spirit of Mrs. Flinnigan, I stuffed old nylon stockings in my shirt to make breasts ("fat ribs"), but Joey didn't get it. He asked, "How come you're fat, Ma, and I'm not?"

80

When I went to Joey's to play, I always went the same way: cross Section Street, walk north on Eleventh to Harris' corner, turn right up Skagit Street until I got to Joey's house. One day Mom suggested that I go around the block the other way and told me how to do it. "Where will I be?" I wondered nervously, fearing I might get lost. "Just do what I said, and you'll see," she replied. "Be sure not to cross any streets and you'll be fine." So I did, and soon I turned a corner and there was Joey's house, just where it had always been, but my little world had suddenly expanded.

When Halloween arrived I was too small to go trick-or-treating. Mom made up little packets of waxed paper tied with string. Each packet contained a couple of cookies, candy corn, and a few pieces of hard candy. The next day she had a couple of packets left over, and she told Joey and me we could play trick-or-treat like the bigger kids. She said to go outside and play for a while and then ring the doorbell. We waited as long as we could and then rang the bell. Mom came to the door, and we waited for the treats.

"Please?" I finally asked.

She prompted, "Trick..."

"Trick-or-treat!" we shouted and like magic, we got our treats. We felt silly to have forgotten what to say.

Another time when there was snow on the ground Joey and I were outside wearing our dark blue snowsuits. We had the hoods up and nothing showed except our eyes, noses, and mouths. My brown hair and Joey's blond hair were completely hidden. We got the idea that if we traded jackets, which had different decorative designs, people would think I was Joey and Joey was me. We walked down the block to the Wright's house and went into the little grove of trees surrounding the fishpond--this must have been before the near-drowning or we wouldn't have dared go in there--where we exchanged jackets, buttoned them up with difficulty (boys' and girls' jackets buttoned on opposite sides, I found out), and put up the hoods. We walked back to my house and rang the doorbell. After a while Mom opened the door. She just looked at us and finally said, "Well, why didn't you just come on in? The door's not locked." She didn't seem to notice that I was Joey and Joey was me.

Finally I said, "Who am I?" but she didn't get it. "Do you think I'm Joey?" I hinted.

"Why would I think you're Joey? I'm busy washing clothes downstairs," she said. "Either come in or stay out, but don't stand there with the door open," and she turned and walked away. "And don't ring the doorbell again!" What a disappointment!

After Joey's family moved to the house attached to the little store by

Lincoln School, the Traunum family bought their old house. They had four children, all older than I, the youngest being Dean, just a year ahead of me in school. His sisters, who slept in one big bedroom upstairs, were Beverly (who played the violin and was too old to play with me); Joanne (who played the piano and fell in the gym at school and knocked out her front teeth); and Paula (who played the clarinet and in the summer organized activities in their backyard, which neighbor girls were invited to join--but only after Paula and her sisters had finished their house work). One such activity was creating elaborate playhouses by throwing blankets over the clotheslines to make walls and rooms.

Mr. Traunum was vice-principal (actually acting principal) at Lincoln School, so he walked to work. Walking was not easy for him, however. He had had polio, and one leg was shorter than the other. Nevertheless, he walked to school and back every day, and up and down its halls. Some kids said that when boys got sent to the office to see Mr. Traunum, he sometimes beat them with a hose. Mr. Traunum always seemed like a nice man to me, but I was just a little leery of him because of those rumors. When I graduated from the eighth grade, it was Mr. Traunum who announced my name, shook my hand, and handed me my diploma.

Beyond the Kenna/Traunum house, at the corner of Skagit and Twelfth Streets, lived the Wynstras. Mr. Wynstra was superintendant of schools, Nancy Wynstra was my age, and when we got old enough to be in Blue Birds (a younger version of Campfire Girls), Mrs. Wynstra was our leader. She asked Mom to be assistant leader, though Nancy said loudly several times that she wanted Mrs. Peterson, Sharon's mother, to be assistant leader. That was in third grade, when Nancy and Sharon, who lived across Twelfth Street from Nancy, were best friends and I was odd-girl out. Later Sharon and I were best friends and Nancy became odd-girl out.

Something was always going on at the Traunums' or Wynstras'. I remember playing statue on the Wynstras' lawn one late summer evening; another time Mrs. Wynstra organized a Halloween party in their basement. Their family took me on outings, and my family took Nancy, so we would have someone to play with. Nancy wasn't an only child, as I was, but her brother Scott was fourteen years older than she and away at college. Nancy, Sharon and I went to Bible school along with the Traunum girls at their Lutheran Church, and we took the YMCA's free swimming lessons the summer we were eight, and more swimming lessons at Clear Lake, out in the country. We started piano lessons at the same time, third grade, and most of all we lived and breathed horses.

The horse craze began in third grade, when Corrine Whitnall came to Lincoln School in a wheelchair, recovering from polio. Corrine loved horses, and soon she was able to gallop around the school yard on crutches and one good leg, while the other girls in class galloped behind her, whinnying and pawing the ground with one foot. Every day after school and after practicing the piano, Sharon, Nancy, and I played horses until suppertime.

Sharon Peterson, first my rival and later my best friend, had a brother one year older, with red hair and freckles, named Lee. The family was Very Religious. They went to church twice on Sunday, besides Sunday School and Bible School in the summer. Mr. Peterson rode to work on a motorcycle with his Bible strapped on the back; and when she was outside hanging washing or feeding the dogs, Mrs. Peterson sang hymns in a strong soprano voice that could be heard all over the neighborhood. The Petersons raised Pekingese dogs for money, breeding Tinker (the female) and Ching (the male). Some neighbors complained that the dogs barked all night.

On both sides of Peterson's house were vacant lots with trees and brush which we referred to as "Peterson's woods." A maze of paths ran

through the woods, and there was even an old tipped over outhouse. The woods were a favorite place to play. Various neighborhood children played horses, hide and seek, and other games there. The summer after third grade Sharon's family took the train to Detroit where they picked up a new DeSoto and drove back across the country, stopping in Indiana to fill a cardboard box with terrapins which Sharon and Lee sold around the neighborhood when they got back. I named mine Terry and made a pen for him outside under the kitchen windows. I put an overturned shoebox in the pen and cut a little opening so he could get out of the sun. One day it rained, softening the cardboard, and apparently Terry got a toe hold and escaped. I heard much later that the Greers, two blocks away, found a terrapin in their

83

yard, but by then I didn't care. There is a picture of me holding Terry, taken just before Mom cut off my long braids. After Daddy took the picture I ran inside, eager for my transformation from freak with braids to normal girl with short hair. Mom, who had been watching from inside, marched me right back out. "Now take another picture," she said to Daddy, "and this time have her braids hanging in front so they show."

Unless it was raining, most of the summer Nancy, Sharon and I ran around barefoot. I even ran up and down on the gravel in the alley to toughen up my feet. One day when Sharon, Nancy and I were wondering what to do next, Sharon absent-mindedly curled her toes so that the big toe on one foot stood straight up while the others curled downward. Then she did the same thing with the other foot and walked around like that for a bit. Nancy was able to do the same thing. Though I tried, I simply could not get my big toes to stand up straight. This was a new experience. Usually I mastered such accomplishments with very little effort, having the attitude that if I couldn't do something easily, then it wasn't important. But this was! It would never do that Nancy and Sharon could do this and I could not. From then on, wherever I was, I tried and tried to raise my big toes. Sunday came and the house was full of relatives, having returned from a picnic earlier in the day. As I stood around working and working at raising a big toe, suddenly one of them popped up! I had done it! Now that I knew what it felt like, I tried to raise the big toe on the other foot and voila! up it popped. What a relief! I messed around some more and figured out how to lower my big toes while the little toes stayed in place. Undoubtedly I demonstrated this feat to Nancy and Sharon as soon as possible. Whether or not it impressed them I don't recall, but it certainly did wonders for my self esteem.

Sharon was basically fearless. When we were visiting horses (there were a few pastured within walking distance) I was content to pull some grass and reach through the fence to feed the animal. But Sharon thought nothing of crawling through the fence and walking all around the horse, or running with a handful of grass trying to get the horse to follow her and gallop. One horse tried to bite her in the middle of the back; it left a mark but didn't break the skin, and it didn't seem to bother her much. Near Hillcrest Park was a gulch with a fallen tree that crossed the gulch perhaps ten or fifteen feet above the deepest part. Sharon scampered back and forth on the tree trunk, no more than a foot in diameter, from one side of the gulch to the other. Since she did it, I had to. There was nothing to hold onto until about halfway across, when a couple of smaller trees rose up close to the fallen tree. I held my breath until I got there, then took another breath and continued to the far side of the gulch.

Then I had to go back. Though I made it across and back safely, my journey was not the carefree trip Sharon made. I was glad my mother never found out about it.

South of Sharon's house, in a small wooden house on the corner of Twelfth and Section Streets, lived Mrs. Bush, Barbie Bush, and Barbie's little brother. Mr. Bush had been killed in an accident driving his milk delivery truck. Barbie Bush was three or four years younger than Nancy, Sharon, and I, and she was fat, all of which made her fair game for pranks and cruelty. We never let her play with us, except once. First we dug a big hole in the middle of the trail through Peterson's woods. Then we filled it with rotten apples and rose bush canes with lots of stickers. Finally, we covered it with branches and scattered dead leaves on top. Once the trap was ready, we went for Barbie. We spoke sweetly to her and invited her to play with us, to come for a walk in the woods. Barbie came smiling, delighted to be accepted at last. Since the three of us were barefoot, it was easy to persuade Barbie to take off her shoes. Sharon led the way, followed by Nancy, then Barbie, with me bringing up the rear. When Sharon came to the trap, she stepped around it, and then Nancy stepped around it and turned to watch Barbie. Barbie stepped just where Nancy and Sharon had stepped, so Nancy pushed her back toward the trap, and I blocked her escape from behind. Still she didn't step into the trap, so Nancy grabbed one leg and tried to force Barbie's foot into the stickers and rotten apples. By then Barbie was shrieking, so we let her escape and run home.

I imagine it was shortly after that episode that I was at Sharon's one morning when Mrs. Bush came over to visit Mrs. Peterson. They went into the bedroom, but even with the door closed Sharon and I could hear them crying. Mrs. Bush was crying about her dead husband and how mean all the kids were to Barbie; and Mrs. Peterson was crying about Mr. Peterson's other women and how mean her kids were to Barbie. Once she came out to get another box of tissues so they could continue crying. She didn't even notice Sharon and me, giggling and poking each other, embarrassed and maybe feeling a tiny bit guilty.

Once when we were outside playing we saw Mr. and Mrs. Peterson in the kitchen with their arms around each other, kissing a long, movie star kiss. Another time when Sharon and I were in the kitchen and Mrs. Peterson was lying on the couch, I ran in to ask her if Sharon could go somewhere with me. Mrs. Peterson had tears on her face and brushed them away as she answered. And one morning when I had come over to play and had to wait in the living room until Sharon finished the dishes, I could hear her quietly crying while her Aunt Georgie tried to comfort her but didn't know how. "You're a funny kid," she said.

The Petersons had begun having trouble when we were in fourth grade because Mr. Peterson chased women, and for a while Mrs. Peterson took Sharon and Lee to Omak where they lived with relatives; eventually they came back but at the beginning of fifth grade the family moved to Bellevue to start over. Mr. Peterson chased women in Bellevue too, however, and eventually the Petersons were divorced.

On the corner of Thirteenth and Section, almost out of my range, was Annaly's house. I remember her from first grade on, though she claimed we knew each other before then. We played together occasionally, though I didn't like her very much. She was fat and used big words like an adult. However, in second grade she was the first friend to stay overnight with me. She brought her Teddy Bear and had asthma in the middle of the night. Annaly wasn't interested in horses or climbing trees, so we didn't really become good friends until eight grade when we were both in Miss Colouzis' room and usually walked home together, Annaly lugging her cello.

Back in Auntie Ruth's block, across 12th Street from the Petersons', just south of the Wynstras, lived Mrs. Dykers and her grownup daughter, Martha, a nurse. Martha had a niece (Mrs. Dykers' granddaughter) who lived on Whidbey Island but visited her grandmother and Aunt Martha often and played with Nancy and hence with me. Her name was Alice Bolster. Alice was a quiet, gentle little girl who liked to play with dolls, as did Nancy. I preferred playing horses and climbing trees, so I wasn't very interested in Alice until she became locally famous. Alice had been born a "blue baby" with a defective heart and at birth was so small she "could fit inside a shoe box," as she was fond of saying. When she was seven years old, she had a heart attack, which made me even less inclined to play with her; I was afraid she might drop dead wheeling her doll buggy down the sidewalk.

Then a miracle happened: Alice became one of the first children in the country to have heart surgery. The operation was very risky, but if successful Alice would be able to live a normal life. Mothers talked with serious faces. Children whispered and felt scared. And then one day Mom told me that Alice's operation was over with, and that she was going to be all right. It was like the sun came from behind a cloud, and even though I wasn't close to Alice, still, she was a kid like me, a kid I knew, a kid who might die, but now she was going to live!

Alice came to her grandmother's house to recuperate. After a while she was allowed to have visitors, and Nancy and I went to see her. She was propped up in bed, weak but smiling, with stacks of books around her and a little bell to ring to summon her grandmother. She wasn't allowed to call loudly yet, and it would be a long recovery, but the recovery would be complete. I always remained a bit in awe of Alice, however, for what she had gone through.

When we were about thirteen I persuaded Alice to go with me on the sledgehammer ride at a carnival downtown. The ride consisted of a capsule to sit inside and a long metal arm attached at one end to the capsule and at the other to a sort of vertical piling. When activated, the capsule began to swing back and forth, higher and higher, and eventually made a complete circle over the top of the piling where it was attached. Then it went around and around before finally slowing down and stopping. As soon as the capsule began to move Alice started to moan. She was frightened to death, and so was I for fear that she would have another heart attack. I screamed for the attendant to stop, but he ignored us. Annaly, waiting at the bottom, knew something was wrong. When the attendant stopped the capsule upside down at the top of its arc (normally the most thrilling part of the ride), I screamed to Annaly to make him let us out. Arguing with Annaly was like arguing with an avalanche, and so, reluctantly the operator cut our ride short and Alice survived. Years later, when I recounted this incident to Alice, she had no memory of it at all.

Continuing south on Twelfth Street from Mrs. Dykers' house there was a vacant lot, then the house at the corner. Before I was in school, Lonnie and I used to play in the vacant lot, which was across the alley from Auntie Ruth's backyard. Eventually a house was built there and was first occupied by the S. family. Their children were too young for me to play with, but one, Suzy, was a friend of my cousin Kay's. Mrs. S. had been born into a rich Seattle family and married a promising young banker. But then she converted to Catholicism, was disowned by her rich family, and proceeded to

With Kay and Nancy Wynstra on dirt from basement of new house being built

have a lot of children whom she didn't know how to take care of. Auntie

87

Ruth was her substitute mother/confidante, trying to teach her how to care for her growing brood without the help of servants. Mrs. S. meant well but lived in a haze of religious devotion, according to Auntie Ruth, unaware that the baby needed changing and that for supper to be on the table before bedtime required some planning and preparation.

Later the P. family lived there, and Mrs. P. was in the same boat when it came to homemaking. She was older than Mrs. S. and had two children older than I was, but she had never had to take care of a house. Her husband was a psychiatrist, and previously the family had lived on the grounds of one or another state mental hospital where housekeepers and groundskeepers were provided. So Auntie Ruth continued her role of mentor for untrained homemakers.

The house on the corner of the block, at Twelfth and Section, belonged to the Thomas family in my early years. Their children were grown. When they moved, the W. family purchased the house. They had one son, Jerry, who was Kay's age. Mrs. W. had led a sheltered life before her marriage. According to Auntie Ruth, her husband had to take her for a walk and show her how the dogs "did it" so she would have some idea what he expected of her. The result was Jerry, whom she protected beyond reason. She was horrified when he came home from Auntie Ruth's one day and announced that he had watched Snooky give birth to three kittens in a built-in drawer in the bedroom off the kitchen. She couldn't believe that Auntie Ruth had been in the kitchen all the time and allowed half the neighborhood children, myself included, to watch the disgusting process. When I was in junior high I sometimes babysat for Jerry. He was fascinated with sports and entertained himself by playing an imaginary baseball game, taking the parts of the various players for the pitch, swing, run, slide, throw, catch, etc. In one way it made babysitting easy, because I didn't have to do anything to entertain him. On the other hand, I had to watch Jerry and react in a way that he thought appropriate, and the kid never seemed to wind down.

OUR BLOCK AGAIN

Back in our block, for a short while Lonnie's family lived in the McClusky house. When they weren't living with the Cannons, they lived in many different houses, which Mr. Varnadore fixed up for the Cannons to sell in their real estate business. Offhand, I can think of at least six houses they occupied in the course of the two or three years that Lonnie and I were playmates. Because I was very interested in houses and curious about their design and interior, I envied Lonnie, getting to live in so many different houses, whereas we never moved even once.

Eventually the Farrell family bought that house and lived there for many years. Their children were younger than I, but their two girls became good friends with our neighbor girls, Gloria and Ann Merryweather. Merrianne, the older Farrell girl, used to hide from her mother by walking into any house with an unlocked door. The first time I laid eyes on her, she was carefully backing into our house via the back door; I could hear her mother's voice faintly calling her from the alley. I asked her what she was doing (I knew who she was, as this habit of hers was well known), but she barely acknowledged me and kept a sharp eye for her mother.

For several years, the Farrell and Merryweather girls put on a summer "show" in the Merryweather back yard. They lined up two or three rows of chairs for the audience on one side of the clotheslines, to which they pinned blankets to form a curtain. Before the show, the girls walked among the audience selling popcorn. When the show started they pulled down the blankets to reveal the stage--the rest of the backyard. There were pantomimes and dances, recitations, songs, and tricks. These included a hula hoop contest, and Maureen riding her tricycle around on the lawn with Ann standing on the back and pushing when necessary. The finale was a play involving a princess. My favorite line concerned the hidden jewel. Whoever found it got to marry the princess, and Gloria, playing the dauntless hero, relied on brains rather than brawn. She/he wondered, "Hmmm, now where would I hide if I were a jewel?" I was in college by this time and found the show to be hysterically funny. Some adults thought I was quite rude, but the kids loved it and afterwards always planned their show for when I would be home to see it.

Beyond the Farrell's house on Twelfth street was a little house set back from the street and similar to the one Ed and Nina and later the Merryweathers had lived in before building their big house. An old lady named Mrs. Lindquist lived there at first. Then, when I was in fourth grade, her son and his family moved in just for a year. They had two girls, Kathy and Margaret Jean, and Kathy was in my grade at Lincoln School and joined our Blue Bird group. Kathy's father had a job in Seattle, so he was only home on weekends. Soon Kathy and I became friends. We stayed overnight with each other, roller skated after school, and when snow came we made snow forts, both in Kathy's yard and in mine. The snow stayed a long time, and one day while playing in Kathy's backyard we decided to make snow people. She made a snow man and I made a snow woman (with breasts to make the distinction and curly hair, represented by little snowballs all over her head). The next day when I went over to play, I saw that my snow woman was broken to pieces. Kathy must have done it out of jealousy because my snow woman was more creative than her snow man, I reasoned, so to get even I trampled her snow fort and went home without knocking on the door. Later I decided to go back anyway, but before I even got to the alley I discovered that someone--Kathy of course--had trampled my snow fort. Somehow we got it straightened out and I learned that Kathy had not ruined my snow lady on purpose; she had tried to move it and it broke apart accidentally. So all was forgiven.

Or almost. In the spring, when the two of us were taking turns with a jump rope, I idly wondered if I stuck out my foot would Kathy fall and break her arm? I didn't consciously want to hurt her. I was just curious. I stuck out my foot, and Kathy fell and broke her arm. Like a good little girl, I walked her home while she howled. A couple of days later Kathy came to school with her arm in a cast, which I signed along with others in the class. For years I never told a soul that I had broken Kathy Lindquist's arm.

Except for a brick house, the rest of the houses on Twelfth street in our block were of no account for me--no kids to play with. Once, though, Kathy and I had an encounter with the man living in the house on the corner at the end of the block. We were roller skating, and the smooth, paved walkway to the front steps was too inviting to ignore. I went first and was about to execute a semi-circle turn when the front door opened and the man yelled to get off his property and stay off! That was one house I skipped when selling Campfire mints.

During the summer before fourth grade I heard from kids in the neighborhood that a Dutch family, just arrived from Holland, had moved into the brick house. When school started, I learned that the girl, Elly, was in my room! Elly had three brothers, long honey-colored sausage curls, and could not speak a word of English. All the girls were fascinated with her and wanted to be friends in spite of the language problem, and when she joined our Blue Bird group we were delighted. At first, Elly would hide her head in her arms, partly laughing and partly crying in frustration because she couldn't understand. Somehow we played together anyway. She learned to jump rope, and she showed us what Dutch girls did instead: they juggled! She could juggle three balls at once, and try as I might, I could only juggle two. Then, all of a sudden it seemed, Elly could speak English! She had an accent, and her sentence structure wasn't always right, but every day she improved. "How you say....," she would begin, and we would supply a new word for her. Many years later I wrote a poem about her:

Elly in Hyacinths

She came to fourth grade from Holland.
In Petersons' woods we played hide and seek.
We built a snow fort in her yard, a snow
Family in mine. Their living room, kept
Closed and unheated, held a spinning wheel.

In spring she came to school in hyacinths,
Fragrant pastel blossoms on strings:
A garland of hyacinths in her hair,
Exquisitely delicate necklaces,
Bracelets on her wrists and ankles.

After school we sat on her back steps making
Strings of hyacinths, choosing carefully
From the carton of wilting blossoms
Her father had brought from the fields.

With Kathy, Elly, Nancy and Sharon all in the neighborhood I always had someone to play with, and often we all played together--a herd of horses galloping through Peterson's woods. Then, in the summer between fourth and fifth grades, every one of them moved away. Nancy's family moved to Kent, south of Seattle. Sharon's family moved to Bellevue, which at that time was a small town near Seattle, on the east shore of Lake Washington. Kathy's family moved to Medina, another small community near Bellevue. And Elly's family moved to a farm on the Britt Slough Road. Suddenly my little group of neighborhood girl friends was gone. Nancy and Kathy and I wrote letters for a while. Sharon and I wrote letters and spent time together in the summer and during school vacations until we were in high school. And Elly and I phoned each other every Friday evening and stayed overnight and visited each other for several years.

Though the fourth grade friendships continued, some longer than others, through letters and occasional visits, the end of fourth grade spelled the end of one phase of my childhood.

MONKEY BARS AND SUCH

After my neighborhood friends moved away and there was no one to play horses with, I discovered a new outdoor interest: monkey bars-- playground equipment for human monkeys consisting of overhead ladders, horizontal bars of various heights, rings hanging from chains, trapezes and other equipment used in gymnastics. Both the Lincoln School playground, one block north of our house, and Hillcrest Park, two blocks to the south, installed monkey bars about this time.

I spent many hours playing on this equipment during fifth and sixth grades, the loneliest two years of my childhood. My hands consistently sported blisters from swinging along the overhead ladders. Sometimes I jumped from one end of the ladder to a rung toward the middle, and more than once landed face down on the dirt below. I considered myself an acrobat and thought about joining a circus.

Meanwhile, I practiced at every opportunity, including during school recess, using the monkey bars like those shown in the diagram below. Hooking one leg over the bar, I learned to turn over and over,

forward and backward without stopping, while the other girls played kick ball or squares. The skin behind my right knee got raw and sore, so I learned to use my left leg instead. Alternating legs worked fairly well, though the skin behind either knee never completely healed before I started using it again. All this was fine in fifth grade, but in sixth grade when a young and pretty new teacher, Mrs. Howard, had playground duty I got in trouble. I must admit she had a point, because of course girls had to wear skirts to school, and my panties showed sometimes. The first time she got after me I quit until she was no longer on playground duty. When none of the other teachers said anything I went back to my old routine and didn't notice when Mrs. Howard was on duty again--until she came storming at me, red in the face, and sent me inside.

I was in my twenties when a classmate from that time told me that Mrs. Howard didn't stop with sending me in from recess. Apparently the boys were gone on some activity elsewhere, and I was sent on an errand to get me out of the classroom so she could address the girls in my room. She asked them to be especially nice to me because I was a troubled child looking for attention. When I learned of this from my former classmate, I was horrified and asked her how she had reacted. Fortunately, she and the other girls didn't think anything was wrong with

92

me and pretty much ignored Mrs. Howard's dire warnings. Years later I learned that Mrs. Howard had eventually committed suicide. I wonder, when she labeled me a troubled child, how troubled she was herself.

By seventh grade I made up my mind to stop grieving for my lost friends, though Sharon and I still corresponded regularly, to stop being such a tomboy, and to try to be like other girls. Two things helped with this. For one, a new girl, Patricia Davis, was in my seventh grade home room. She was cute and nice, and before long we became best friends. The other helpful thing was that the new P.E. teacher, Miss Watson, introduced us to tumbling, which was sort of like playing on the monkey bars, and I was very good at it. Finally a teacher approved of my physical accomplishments.

However, I wasn't very good at chinning myself, which I tried not only on the monkey bars but also hanging from the doorway moldings at home, and I never mastered walking on my hands for more than three or four "steps." However, I learned to stand on my head, and I taught myself to turn very good cartwheels. My greatest accomplishment along these lines was learning to do a flip, which Daddy called a hand-spring. After numerous failures I finally mastered the process of running fast, putting both hands on the ground, and flipping over, landing on my feet. This accomplishment paid off in eighth grade when I was elected cheer leader, though I never learned to flip over without using my hands. Interestingly, though the five cheer leaders wore skirts and blouses, and two of us did flips as part of our routines, no authority figures seemed to object. Maybe because by then the style was to wear two or three stiff, frilly crinoline petticoats under our full skirts, probably camouflaging the panties.

THE TOWN

We lived near the south end of Lincoln Hill, which marked the east end of the Skagit River delta. The hill was really a rolling clay plain which continued east to Big Lake and foothills of the Cascade Range. Eleventh Street, twelve blocks long, ran from the high school at its north end to Hillcrest Park in the south. Our house, at 1204 South Eleventh, was two blocks from the park. Beyond the park, the Blackburn Road marked the city limits when I was a child.

There is a picture of my father and me sitting on a small log that partly formed a low fence at the edge of the park. Daddy used a timer to

take the picture one sunny fall day. I look to be going on two years old and remember being uneasy sitting by myself while he set the timer.

Afterwards we walked through a carpet of fallen leaves, and later he made that into a remember-when bedtime story with the words, "rustle, rustle, rustle." Peacocks, which lived in a large pen made of chicken wire, spread their tails to impress onlookers and cried "help," a sound like a woman screaming. I could hear it at night from my bedroom. Set among fir trees, the park had a couple of picnic shelters, a wading pool, swings, and two teeter-totters made of three-inch thick planks. Later a slide and monkey bars were added. One day Lonnie's mother took us to the park to play on this new equipment. While Mrs.

Varnadore sat on a bench smoking and thumbing through a magazine, I demonstrated the slide for Lonnie, then climbed up behind him so he wouldn't be scared. Lonnie sat at the top and slid down just as I'd shown him, but at the bottom he shot off the end and landed hard on his bottom, not realizing he had to put his feet down. He howled and his mother came running. I felt bad that I hadn't pointed out how to get off the slide.

I didn't know the park had a name. One day I was riding my bike (on the sidewalk, as instructed), when two men in a truck stopped to ask if I could tell them where Hillcrest Park was. I was nervous, thinking these might be the Boogymen Grandma worried about. I said, "You mean Mount Vernon park?" They nodded, I told them, and they drove off. That's how I learned the park had a name.

Across the road from the picnic and playground area were tennis courts and the Hillcrest Lodge. One Easter Daddy took me to an Easter egg hunt, which began on the tennis courts. When the talking stopped the kids started running toward the main area of the park to find the eggs. I was too little to keep up with the bigger kids, who grabbed eggs right and left before I could get to them. Even Daddy couldn't find any after that, and finally he complained to one of the men in charge, who showed us where to look under a certain bush, and there I found my one and only egg. Another Easter morning, when I was in the eighth grade, Mom, my then best friend Patricia, and I went to sunrise services on the tennis courts. Everybody had to stand; it was cold and had been raining. I was not inspired. Later, before

Patricia and I attended services at the Baptist Church, where I sincerely tried to make sense of the sermon, Daddy took our picture in our Easter finery standing on the sidewalk beside our blooming crabapple tree. My eyes are closed and the sidewalk is wet.

Built by the CCC during the Depression, Hillcrest Lodge was a one-story building made of logs. During elections the lodge became the voting place for our precinct. For many years, once I was in school, Mom worked there representing the Democrats, while Mrs. Cook, my classmate Connie's mother, represented the Republicans. The lodge was the site of weddings, receptions, high school reunions, and on a rainy day when I was in the eighth grade, our class picnic. For seven years classmates and I had walked from Lincoln School to the park for a picnic in May, then played there the rest of the afternoon before walking back to school for dismissal. Mom, and sometimes Grandma, always watched for us and waved as we marched to the park. When the eighth grade picnic was rained out, the four eighth grade classes, amounting to about 120 students plus teachers, crammed into the lodge. My class, taught by Miss Colouzis, was the only one which had fried chicken, purchased from fines of five cents apiece levied against anyone caught chewing gum in class. The other three classes had to settle for sack lunches. After lunch we played games, including charades. Mrs. Nordine's class stumped the rest of us with their charade. They just stood there, pointed to the floor, then spread their arms wide. The answer: "From Here to Eternity," the title of a recent movie which I was not allowed to see.

Hillcrest Park Lodge

The eighth grade graduation party, which my parents helped chaperone, was held at the Hillcrest Lodge. All students who would begin high school the next fall were invited. Besides the four classes from Lincoln School, there were students from the Catholic school, the Christian Reformed school, and Conway public school. Norman Etherington, future valedictorian, who had a crush on Patricia, followed her everywhere while she tried to avoid him. We danced to records played on a portable phonograph, and I wrote in my diary that I danced every dance with Jimmy Thomson including the last dance, "Sincerely," sung by the Maguire Sisters.

To get downtown from our house we drove or walked down the hill on Broad Street. Wells' Nursery was at the bottom on the left (south), where Broad Street turned due west and became West Kincaid. To the north from the bottom of the hill was a marshy area. When I was very

96

young Grandma lived just east of the grain elevator in a house against the side of the hill. We could take a shortcut through the marsh, walking on boards in some areas, to her house. Today the grain elevator still stands, but the marsh, most of Wells Nursery, and Grandma's house are covered by Interstate 5. Sometimes Grandma took care of me in this house, when Mom worked as a substitute at the telephone office. The only time I saw her oldest sister, Great Aunt Belle, was at that house, when she was visiting from Canada. Grandma showed me off, asking me to "dance," which amounted to whirling around and waving my arms. This was during the War, and another "cute" thing I did to entertain Aunt Belle and the other sisters was to make, I regret to say, a "Jap" face--screwing up my face trying to look as ugly as possible. Grandma lived on the main floor of this house, and she rented the upstairs to a very old woman named Mrs. Snyder, about whom I wrote a rhyme many years later:

> Mrs. Snyder, like a spider
> Hunched and creeping up the stairs

Once for lunch Grandma fixed hot tamales, which I found inedible. I haven't had one since. She drank tea for lunch and told my fortune with the tea leaves left in the cup.

Skagit County Courthouse   If , at the bottom of Lincoln Hill, we didn't go to Grandma's, we continued past the lumber yard (source of the fearsome yardstick), crossed the railroad tracks (I remember steam locomotives, which Daddy explained in detail as we waited at the crossing by the depot), and passed the courthouse that he had helped build. Two Civil War canons stood in front.

The downtown area consisted of Main Street, the street closest to the Skagit River where the town first began; First Street, the primary shopping street; and Second Street, also Highway 99, site of other businesses. These streets ran parallel to the Skagit River in a north-northeast to south-southwest direction.

At the south end of Main Street was the Moose Hall, right on the river, and next to it, attached to a pier, a vertical device measured the height of the river. At its north end Main Street met Division Street, running east and west and crossing on a bridge to the West Side. Across Division to the north was the Carnation Condensery, with its smokestack and whistle which punctuated the work day. During all of my growing-up years, the whistle marked the hours, Monday through Friday. It could be heard all over town and into the surrounding countryside. The first whistle of the day came at 7:55 a.m.--two short blasts to signal that work was about to begin. At 8:00 came a longer single blast, start of the morning shift. Another long blast at noon signaled the beginning of lunch hour. At 12:55 came the warning blasts, and at 1 p.m. another long blast to begin the afternoon shift. The final blast of the day, at 5 p.m., indicated the end of the work day. At the 8 a.m. blast I was just getting up. At noon, if I happened to be playing somewhere in the neighborhood, the blast meant it was time to go home for lunch. Later, when I worked in the fields west of town during high school summers, the noon whistle was the signal for lunch under the shade trees. On those days, at the 5 p.m. blast I was just getting into the bathtub to wash off the day's accumulation of dirt.

There were a few businesses on Main Street, the biggest of which was Bert Robinson's store, which sold hardware, fishing equipment, and other things I wasn't interested in. After the town got a radio station, KBRC, every weekday from noon until 1 p.m. "The Farmer's Exchange" program was broadcast from the store, presenting news from "The rich and fertile Skagit Valley." The program was of little interest to me except for one summer day when Sharon, who had moved to Bellevue, was visiting. We were eating lunch when the radio announced that the store was giving away free balloons to any kids who came in during the broadcast. We gobbled down the rest of our lunch and ran all the way down the hill, through town and on to the store. The announcer, who was still on the air, saw us and said, "Hello, girls, come get your free balloons." We were thrilled; it was almost like being on the radio ourselves. As we walked back up the hill we discussed what to do with these special balloons, and by the time we got to Lincoln School we had it figured out. We tied the strings of our helium-filled balloons together, let them go, and held hands until they were out of sight. Friends forever.

Other buildings on Main Street housed Collins Office Supply, the bus station, and the Mission Theater, which became the Lyric Theater about the time I was in seventh grade. June's Grocery, between Bert

98

Robinson's and the West Side bridge, was where my folks did their weekly grocery shopping after Stewart's Grocery, on First Street, stopped making home deliveries. While my folks shopped I read comics and movie magazines at the news stand and watched the donut machine plop dough into hot grease. A parade of donuts circled around, got turned by a little automatic flipper, circled again, and finally traveled up a conveyer ramp, all cooked and ready for the donut lady to decorate. Our weekly groceries usually cost a little over ten dollars. One summer, June's and other local businesses participated in a raffle. For each ten dollars spent, customers got one raffle ticket. The drawing, the grand prize being a brand new pea green Buick sedan, was held at the Fairgrounds around Labor Day. We lost.

The south end of First Street began at the cold storage business, where we had a locker. Everyone who could afford it had a locker. After the War people began to get home freezers or refrigerators with freezing compartments on top, but the cold storage business continued to operate for many years. Heavy wooden doors opened to two separate sections of lockers. When Daddy opened the door to our section we stepped into a cold, frosty room lined with aisles of lockers on two

First Street, looking north--1940's

levels. The walls, ceilings and pipes were all covered with thick white frost. I'm not sure what we kept in our locker other than berries and perhaps other fruit and vegetables that didn't do so well if home-canned. Frozen items were stored in round, red and white pint- or quart-sized waxed cartons with lids.

At the north end of First Street was the Safeway store, where Auntie Ruth shopped. Sometimes Mom and I went with her, wheeling Kay in her baby buggy down the hill and across the tracks, stopping at various

99

stores along the way and ending up at Safeway, where Uncle Del met us and drove us home. By the time I was in high school Safeway had moved to Riverside, and its old location was a parking lot. "Dragging the gut" consisted of driving back and forth on First Street on weekends with a date if you were lucky or a carload of friends if you weren't. The turnaround points were the cold storage building at the south end and the parking lot at the north end.

In between these points were two movie theaters, three or four drug stores, two banks, two bakeries, various clothing stores, a hardware store, several cafes and shoe stores, Sears, Penney's, Montgomery Ward, specialty shops, and The President Hotel where Uncle Roggie worked as night desk clerk The hotel, with five stories, was the tallest building downtown.

The City Bakery and a soda fountain shared an entryway from the sidewalk but had separate doors set at angles. I loved the bakery with its delicious smells and display of baked goods. The several-tiered wedding cakes made my mouth water; I didn't realize for a long time that they were painted cardboard. Occasionally my mother treated me at the soda fountain next door, and once I spilled most of my vanilla milkshake down the length of the counter. Mom was embarrassed and I almost cried, but the soda jerk smiled, made me another milkshake, and acted as if wiping up spilled milkshakes was his favorite part of the job.

Lincoln Theater

The Lincoln Theater was truly a movie palace in its heyday with a large auditorium and a Wurlitzer organ which Daddy coveted. By the time I was going to movies the heyday had passed, but it was still the grandest theater this side of Bellingham. Only once did the organ play when I was in attendance. Several chimes were located at spaced intervals along each side wall, and when the organist struck a chime a light flashed at its top. Our favorite seats were toward the back on the left side, where three seats, located above the entry aisle,

100

had nothing in front of them, so I could always see. We never sat in the three corresponding seats on the right side unless "our" seats were already occupied. It felt funny to sit there. I know I saw *The Best Years of Our Lives* at the Lincoln, because the theater was so crowded that we had to sit on the side in the second row. From that angle everything was distorted, and I marveled at the actors' oddly shaped heads.

I saw part of my first movie at the Lyric Theater, farther down the street. Daddy decided to take me in for a short time so I could see what movies were like. The film was black and white, and all I remember is a man and woman standing under a white archway. We didn't stay long. By the time I was in junior high the Lyric had moved to Main Street where the Mission Theater used to be. A new theater, the Lido, opened where the Lyric had been. It was very modern, with glass doors fronting the street and plush seats that you could push back to let people walk in front of you or to sit up higher if a tall person blocked your view. I don't remember which theater showed *The House of Wax*, the first major studio 3-D film released when I was about twelve. The wax museum's creepy proprietor (Vincent Price) created his lifelike wax figures by immersing real people, whom he had just murdered, into vats of hot wax. Sharon and I saw it together and had to walk home in the dark. We ran all the way. Movies came to town after the first run at the big downtown Seattle theaters. Sometimes we had to wait months after its release to see a popular movie.

The Scamper Shop catered to the well-dressed little girl. It also was one of three stores which sold Jantzen sweaters, the others being Millers and Parkers Men's Shop (with a little corner in the back for women). When I was about seven my mother's cousin Win visited from California and thrilled me by taking me to the Scamper Shop where she bought me two cotton dresses: one with a turquoise top and turquoise-plaid skirt and trim; and the other with a wide pastel plaid pattern. I called it my rainbow dress. By the time I was in fifth grade some classmates were allowed to take home two or three Scamper Shop dresses "on approval." Normally, though, I got clothes at Penney's or Sears, or Mom sewed them for me on her old treadle sewing machine upstairs.

Ann Richards' store sold clothing for the well-dressed woman. The only time I went in there was to look for a formal to wear to a big deal high school dance. Amazingly, I found one! It was a pale blue, lightly quilted, sleeveless sheath, which I wore to at least two dances including the Junior Prom. Other than that, Ann Richards was out of my league. By high school, I tried to avoid Sears and Penney's, which left Warners, Millers, and Parkers. Besides clothing, Warners had the only public restroom downtown, a necessity for me. On the main floor Millers sold dry goods (fabric and whatever else the term implies). The cashier was on the second floor, visible from below through a small window. A series of pneumatic tubes, such as those used today for drive-in banking, ran up to the ceiling from several points on the main floor and across the ceiling to the cashier. When someone made a purchase the clerk put the money and sales slip in a container and, with a loud POP sent it through the tubes to the cashier. In a minute or two it came back, THUMP, with the change. Even in high school, I kept my fingers in my ears until the change came back.

Millers' second floor, accessed via a small elevator, was a good place for women and teenage girls to shop for clothing, including undies, Jantzen sweaters, and formals. When I was in seventh grade, initial pins, which sold for fifty cents apiece at Millers, were worn by every well-dressed girl. I immediately spent my allowance on a J and a G, which I wore on each side of my collar, and at 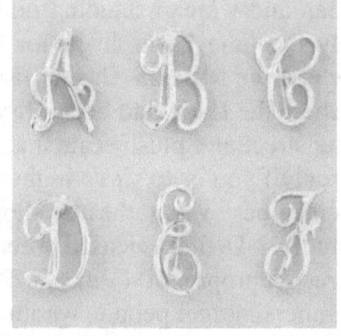 Christmas I bought PD for my new best friend, Patricia Davis. If you had a boyfriend, you traded initial pins. For a while I wore JJ (John Jamieson), but I wasn't entirely happy with JJ, because the two J's weren't identical and I was afraid people would mistake the odd-looking J for a G and not realize I had a boyfriend. I wasn't entirely happy with John Jamieson either, and after a while I got my own pins back and hoped, vainly, to exchange them for SW (Steve Whoolery), worn by Connie Cook at the time.

As a young child I usually had three pairs of shoes: an old pair for playing outside or walking on the beach; a newer everyday pair ("school shoes" later on), for most occasions; and "Sunday School shoes," also worn to parties. When I started school I wanted saddle shoes, but Mom insisted on "a nice pair of Oxfords." The party shoes were always patent leather Mary Janes, which started out black and glossy but ended up with millions of tiny cracks marring their surface. Sometimes bits of the shiny black even peeled off revealing dull black cloth beneath. When I was in grade school the shoe stores invested in the latest thing to insure the best fit possible. This progressive device was an x-ray machine with three viewing windows, which allowed me, Mom, and the salesperson to see the bones in my feet and the outline of the shoes while bombarding all of us with radiation. When I wiggled my toes we all could see how they were straight, with room to grow, and grow they did.

In third grade I was wearing size 5-1/2 shoes, which was great because that was Auntie Claire's size, and she gave me some old pairs of high heels to wear for dress-up. However, I soon outgrew them, and by the end of fifth grade I was wearing size 8-1/2. Fortunately, that turned out to be my adult size, though I kept growing vertically for a few more years, trying to catch up with my feet. It might have been for sixth grade that I got a pair of school shoes that I never wore. They seemed okay when I tried them on in the store. The shoes were tan with crepe soles and a strap across the instep. When I put them on at home, however, they resembled big tan barges. For several years they sat in my closet and finally went to a rummage sale. Many years later Daddy told me that, around the time of the tan barges, someone said that if I ever caught up with my feet I would be six feet tall. That never happened, but my pipe stem legs grew longer and filled out to somewhat offset the size of my feet, though no one has ever called them dainty.

Eventually I got saddle shoes, the standard through junior high and high school. "Soap and water" saddles were preferred except for a short period around eighth grade when "white bucks" were in. These had the same design as saddle shoes but were all white, with a rough, suede-like finish. Regular shoe polish wouldn't work on white bucks; it would ruin the suede finish. So instead we carried around little bags of white powder to pat on the shoes and freshen them up. The powder got on our clothes, especially dark skirts when we forgot and sat on one foot. Eventually, though, the surface became smooth despite constant powdering. Then we took a stiff brush to the white bucks to try to revive the suede.

For eighth grade graduation I got my first pair of high heels. They were white, two inches high at the most, and covered with a kind of rough cloth--very girlish, sort of transition shoes. My next pair of heels were shiny black with really high heels; I wore them to several formal dances. During my senior year "glass heels" (Cinderella slippers) were the rage--open-toed sling-backs with silver paper insoles and clear plastic heels with designs molded into them. I got a pair for the Rainbow Tolo at the Holiday Ballroom. It was pouring rain when we went in and pouring rain when we came out. The dirt parking lot was awash in mud, which oozed into the flimsy shoes. I never wore them again. That wasn't quite enough for me to swear off high heels for life, so when I went off to graduate school as a teaching assistant I wanted to look the part, which meant shopping in Seattle. In the bargain basement at Nordstrom (then just a shoe store) I found a pair of black leather pumps with very high, very thin "stacked" heels (many thin layers of wood). Off I marched to teach the first class of my life at Ohio University, where all the sidewalks were paved with bricks, and the spaces between them grabbed my thin stacked heels with every step. I walked most of the way to class on the balls of my feet and after that wore those shoes mainly on dates and to parties.

Mount Vernon had two five-and-dime stores: Woolworths and Equals Variety Store, owned by the family of Ann Equals, a girl in my dancing class and later in my class at school. I always headed for the toy aisles to look for paper dolls and plastic furniture for my dollhouse. One hot August afternoon I was in Woolworths with Grandma when suddenly the store lights went out. We walked to the front of the store where a salesclerk was pulling down the shades on the glass-fronted doors. In answer to Grandma's question, she smiled and told us the store was closing, that the War was over. Outside, cars drove down the street honking, and people were yelling. We walked home, and just at the top of Lincoln Hill we heard the Carnation whistle begin to blow and blow and blow--even though it was just the middle of the afternoon. As soon as I got home I went over to Auntie Ruth's, skipping along the sidewalk saying to myself, "Hooray! Now we can have nylon stockings!" Other than that, I have few memories of the War: red meat tokens, Mom rolling bandages for the Red Cross, blackout paper on the windows at night, being told to "hush" when news came on the radio, and Daddy coming home from work at the shipyard in La Conner.

Two businesses on First Street closed before I was in school. One was a meat market, with sawdust or wood chips on the floor. It closed when supermarkets put such specialty shops out of business. The other place that closed was Stewart's Grocery. Shoppers stood at the counter and told the clerk what they wanted, and the clerk brought the items to them. I remember mainly canned goods, though I suppose they sold other things such as baking goods and grains. Stewart's also made home deliveries, because most families had just one car and typically went to town just once a week. Mom would call the store and read off her list, and later that day the delivery man came with the items packed in a cardboard box. She was disgusted when Stewart's stopped making deliveries, and shortly after that they closed altogether, another casualty of the supermarket. That's when we started shopping on Saturdays at June's.

Eating places on First Street included the Mount Vernon Cafe, Hoffstee's (which later became Gale's Restaurant, owned by Annaly's cousin), and The Palace Cafe, where Daddy often ate lunch when sanding floors in town. He told a story about a drunk trying to open a package of crackers to put in his soup. The drunk fumbled and fumbled and couldn't get the darn thing open, until finally he crumpled up the package, cellophane and all, threw it in the soup, and walked out. If I walked downtown with a friend after high school, the Mount Vernon Cafe was a favorite spot for a coke, soon followed by a visit to Warners to use the restroom. I don't recall ever eating at Hoffstee's, perhaps because of a story Mom told. Before I was born and she was working at the telephone office, she sometimes ate lunch downtown. She was sitting at the counter at Hoffstee's, waiting for her order, when a cockroach poked its head over the edge of the counter in front of her. She poked her finger at it, and it ducked back down, but soon its head came up again, so she poked again. This exchange repeated itself several times. I don't know if she stayed to eat her lunch that day, but she never went back. Thriftway drug store had a lunch counter, though I never ate there. Aunt Nina Jacobs was the only waitress and went about the job in her typical no-nonsense manner, jerking away customers' plates almost before they finished eating.

Wells Pharmacy was my favorite drug store for several reasons. My mother knew the owner, Paul Wells, from childhood, and his son Robert was in my class at school. The cosmetics counter had all sorts of perfume in atomizers for free samples. The clerk was a very pretty, pleasant woman, Mrs. Haines The store also had a free telephone for customers or just kids who needed a ride home or permission to have dinner with a friend's family. The other drug stores were Stewarts, where I bought my mother the cabbage rose compact, and one owned by Hal Murray, who drowned himself in the river.

Second Street was also Highway 99, with various businesses of little interest to me except for the West Coast Telephone Company, where Aunt Claire was Chief Operator and my mother had worked until I was born. Sometimes Mom went back to work as a substitute when I was very young, or she took me to visit with "the girls" and have coffee in the break room. When I was in seventh grade the phone company finally switched to a dial system, and our phone number changed from 5901 to EDgewater 6-2021. Weeks before the changeover a technician installed the dial in our phone on the kitchen wall. He tied the dial so it couldn't be used until the time was right, which was to be at midnight on a Saturday night. I had just gone to bed around 11 p.m. when Mom called up the stairs, "Janet, we have a dial tone." I leaped out of bed and ran down to hear it for myself. What a thrill! I had been waiting for this day since I was old enough to answer to "number, please." The next day I called Patricia (ED 6-3275), Aunt Claire (ED 6-2020), and Aunt Ruth (ED 6-2932). West Coast Telephone served residences within the city limits. Several months or weeks later, the Rural Telephone Company converted to dials, with a GArfield 4- prefix.

The downtown part of Second Street ended at the viaduct, which went over the railroad tracks to the northern part of the hill. On the west side of Second street, at the bottom of the viaduct, the Rural Telephone Company occupied a tan stucco house. My mother had been born in that house and lived there with my Grandma and Grandpa Ward and Mom's sisters, my Aunt Claire and Barbara's mother, Mary, who died before I was born. At that time Grandma's parents--my great-grandparents--lived on the other side of Second Street. In my day their house was gone, replaced by a laundry. At the top of the viaduct Highway 99 continued north to Riverside, the area between the north end of the hill and the river, which ran from east to west at that point. When my mother was eleven the family moved to Riverside where they had a farm, referred to as "the ranch." Mom lived there until she got married. After Grandpa Ward died Grandma sold the ranch, but the house remained there for many years, as Riverside changed from farmland to urban sprawl. I remember it standing alone on the two-lane highway, and later when it became the office of the Town and Country Motel. Later still it was moved up on the hill and turned around, so the back door became the front door. Whenever we drove past either location Mom looked at the house and sighed.

East of the top of the viaduct was the First Baptist Church, an imposing brick structure where I first met up with religion. My Grandma Grimes had enrolled me in its Nursery Department soon after I was born, and Aunt Ruth and my father, respecting her wishes, saw to it that I got a rudimentary religious education. At first I enjoyed Sunday School, especially in the Beginners Department, where I learned to sing "Jesus Loves Me" and "Jesus Wants Me for a Sunbeam." In order to graduate

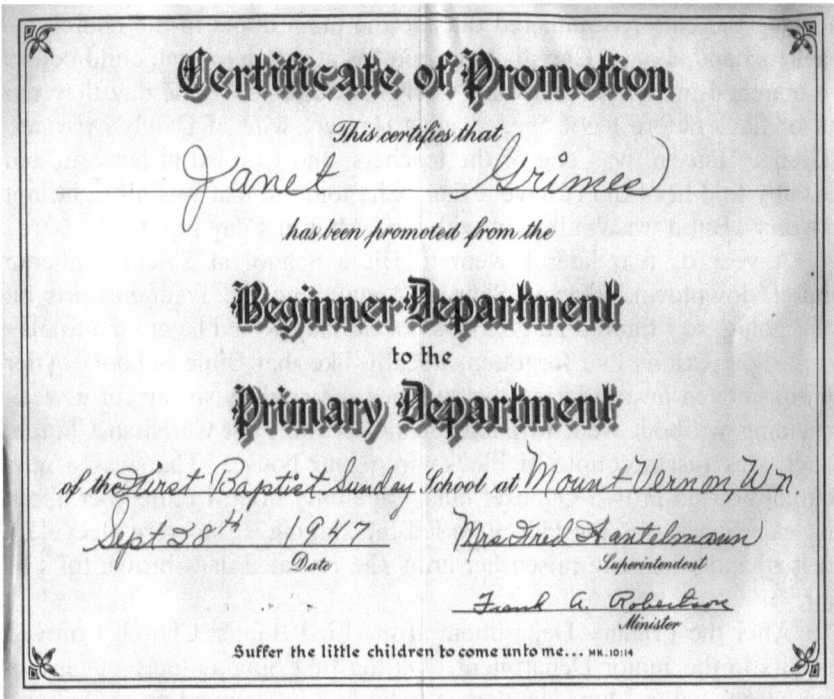

Certificate of Promotion
This certifies that
Janet Grimes
has been promoted from the

Beginner Department
to the

Primary Department

of the First Baptist Sunday School at Mount Vernon, Wn.
Sept 28th 1947
Date
Mrs Fred Hantelmann
Superintendent

Frank A. Robertson
Minister

Suffer the little children to come unto me... MK.10:14

to the Primary Department I had to memorize the twenty-third psalm, a task which I managed but didn't relish. I didn't want to flunk Sunday School and not make it to heaven. In the Primary Department (grades one through three) there were two collection baskets as you walked in, a small red one for the poor missionaries and a larger brown one for the church. I always put my offering in the red basket. Now a bit of work was involved, such as memorizing Bible verses and reciting them. I always tried to volunteer before anyone else recited my favorite verse: "Jesus wept." It was my favorite because it was the shortest. At the end of the hour we marched out to "Onward Christian Soldiers."

When we had a Christmas play I got to be Mary, but on performance night I forgot to bring a doll for the part of baby Jesus. Fortunately, one was rounded up from the Nursery Department. All I had to do was stand up at a certain point during the song the angels, shepherds, Joseph, Wise Men, cows and camels were singing. There were programs at Easter, when I had to recite a poem or part of a narrative. Because I was afraid I would forget my lines, when my turn came I spoke them as fast as I could to get the ordeal over with. Daddy said the words came out so fast he couldn't understand them.

Vacation Bible School never appealed to me. I was supposed to be on vacation! My first experience occurred when I was five or six. Each morning the children gathered outside the main doors to the church, as teachers handed out a Christian or United States flag to each child before we marched in singing "Onward Christian Soldiers." One day they ran out of flags before I got one. Louise Hansen, wife of Daddy's partner, Clarence Hansen, was one of the teachers, and I pulled at her arm and tearfully told her I didn't have a flag. She told me that was all right, not to worry. But it wasn't all right with me. After that day I quit.

A year or two later I went to Bible School at Salem Lutheran Church downtown. Nancy, Sharon, Annaly and the Traunum girls all were going, so I figured I'd go too, since nobody would be around to play with. For reasons I've forgotten, I really like that Bible School. After Sharon moved away, during the summer she could visit me for a week providing we both went to Bible School at the First Christian Church, which was just a couple of blocks from our house. That was a new church, housed in two Quonset huts. The only thing I remember about that experience was the lady who led the singing. She wore sleeveless dresses, and when she raised her arms she revealed dark brown tufts of hair.

After the Primary Department at the First Baptist Church I moved upstairs to the Junior Department. On the first Sunday there our group was introduced to Mary Hantleman, who had just moved on to the next department. Mary stood there as an example of perfect attendance for all three years in the Junior Department. I was not sufficiently inspired. Sunday School was beginning to bore me, and though most of the teachers were very nice, they required more work than I cared to do. My attendance became sporadic and eventually stopped altogether.

When I got to high school I began hearing talk of church groups for teenagers. I was a sophomore when Carol Jean Shrauger persuaded me to go back to the Baptist Church, where the Reverend Wilholland Williams corralled us and asked us to come to Baptist Youth Fellowship on Sunday evenings. Our leaders were a very nice couple, Mr. and Mrs. Vandenberg, and there were two young sailors from Whidbey Island in attendance, as well as a nice boy from Stanwood named Charlie Bean. Charlie, who had a 1947 Ford repainted bright blue, took me to movies and gave me my first kiss. When he was working in Eastern Washington over the summer he wrote me letters and called me long distance twice. In his words, he did "a complete flip" over me. Too bad I didn't flip for him, but by then I was setting my sights on Jim Day, football, basketball and baseball star. Carol Jean flipped for one of the sailors.

Jim Day lived right across the alley from the back side of the church, and one Saturday the BYF group was at the church doing some Christian service chore. Charlie knew I was interested in Jim and began to tease me. Things got out of hand, and pretty soon he and an accomplice were holding my ankles and dangling me headfirst out a second story window, telling me to holler for Jim to rescue me. I was furious and later got even by letting all the air out of Charlie's tires. After that he gave up on me.

I gave up on church shortly thereafter, but not before I finally "went forward" to confess my sins and take Jesus as my personal savior. I had resisted through years of Sunday School, Bible School, and two summers of attending week-long Christian Service Camp on Orcas Island, going only because it was a chance to spend a week with Sharon. Finally I thought, what the heck, so I went forward and was greeted by Reverend Williams, who grasped my hands and solemnly inquired, "How do you come?" After pondering the question I finally responded, "Well, one week I drive and the next week Carol Jean drives." He had to explain

that he meant was I a heathen or a member of some other church.

On a Sunday evening a few weeks later, wearing a shapeless white garment with weights sewn into the hem, I waded into the baptismal tub where Reverend Williams tipped me over backward while I held my nose. I emerged streaming water and saved. Now I could take part in the monthly communion service, which amounted to eating a little square of white bread and sipping a tiny glass of grape juice, passed along the pew in special trays. The issue of communion proved the final straw in my dropping out. At one of our BYF meetings, during a question and answer period, I wondered why Baptists didn't use real wine at communion. In fact, they disapproved of alcohol altogether. I pointed out that Jesus turned water to wine, so he must have thought it was okay. Our leaders, the Vandenbergs, had a ready answer: the Biblical water-to-wine episode was a miracle and occurred instantaneously, whereas wine has to ferment, they explained, so it wasn't real wine, just grape juice. In their view, even Jesus had his limitations.

Two high school friends, Judy Duranceau and Jerry Garrett, lived next door to each other across the street from the main entrance to the church. One warm summer night a car load of us girls were parked in

109

front of Judy's house, waiting for her, while across the street in the parsonage, a light went on in an upstairs window. A visiting minister was staying there while Rev. Williams was out of town, and while we watched he proceeded to strip naked and expose himself to anyone looking his way. Though he must have heard our giggles through the open window, he lingered there long enough for us to get a good eyeful.

Whenever I was driving, after picking Judy up or dropping her off, I would drive around the side of the church and go through Day's alley just for the thrill of passing their house, knowing that Jim might be there. If Carol Jean was in the car, she would try to grab the wheel to make me hit their garbage cans. Fortunately, that never happened. I would have died on the spot--or later when my father saw the car.

Farther east up the hill from the church was the General Hospital, a white wooden building where I was born, Uncle Roggie and Grandpa died, and Grandma recovered from her broken hip. Beyond that was the yellow brick, Spanish style Catholic Church, which could be seen from as far away as the Swinomish Slough to the west. I always thought it looked like a camel from that distance. A little farther along was the Ebeling Clinic.

Before the clinic was built I went to Dr. Crim, a woman. Drs. Ebeling and Mattson, who had delivered me, were the family doctors, and because I was a difficult baby (colicky and nervous), they made regular house calls in my infancy, to the point that any man wearing a hat set me screaming. Finally my parents resorted to Dr. Crim. I remember just two things about her. Her office was upstairs in a building downtown, one of the few which had an elevator. It was about the size of a phone booth and jerked and yanked itself to the second floor with effort. I preferred the stairs, but Mom thought we should use the elevator since it was there. The other thing I remember is getting vaccinated for smallpox. Mom wanted the vaccination to be on my thigh rather than my upper arm because she thought the scar could be unsightly. So I watched as Dr. Crim dabbed a solution on an area about the size of a dime and then pricked the skin very rapidly in a number of places, so fast that I didn't have time to cry. In a few days an ugly scab formed, which eventually dried up and dropped off in a gas station restroom on our way to California, my first trip out of the state.

By the time I broke my ankle, at age seven, Dr. Ebeling had built a clinic on East Division, a couple of blocks up from the Catholic Church and almost around the corner from the house where Grandma lived at that time. Because of the curved glass brick wall by the clinic's front door, I have never cared for glass brick. The mere sight of it used to give me butterflies. What I remember most about the clinic is waiting. First you waited for at least an hour in the large waiting room, with its red ceramic tile floor. Chairs, all occupied, lined three walls. Usually there was at least one crying baby or hyperactive child. Periodically the nurse came to the door and called a name. For several years the nurse was Elizabeth von Moos, a beautiful young woman whom Jimmy Jacobs courted for a while and got engaged to, though they eventually broke up. One time I gave her a picture of Jimmy that I'd taken with my Brownie Hawkeye camera. From the waiting room you proceeded to another space, sometimes no bigger than a closet, where you continued to wait for a minimum of fifteen more minutes. Finally you progressed to one of the three examining rooms, where the nurse stuck a glass thermometer in your mouth and said the doctor would be in shortly. "Shortly" might be another fifteen minutes. Finally the man himself entered wearing a business suit: Dr. Ebeling with his double chin and big belly; Dr. Hammond, with his crooked broken nose; or Dr. Voegtlin, who was said to be very handsome and clearly thought so too, though I thought his features were coarse. The actual examination took maybe five minutes, depending on the complaint. Then the doctor left, you got dressed if you had undressed, and were shown into the doctor's office where you waited again until he came in with the verdict.

Occasionally during this routine I might be sent to the clinic's lab to pee in a cup or provide a blood sample, which was taken from my ear lobe. On a couple of occasions I had x-rays. Besides mainly waiting, in the Ebeling Clinic I got my first and only plaster cast, applied to my lower left leg and foot. It wasn't a break, Dr. Ebeling said, because the ankle bones hadn't yet fused; instead they pulled apart. For a month I wore the cast to the beach, climbing trees, jumping off the foundation of the house Dick Merryweather was building next door, and walking everywhere. Walking casts had not yet been invented, and before it finally came off the bottom was soft, having been worn away from all that walking. The cast was smelly and full of sand, and my filthy leg had shrunk to half the circumference of my other leg, which embarrassed me. I was afraid people would think I was a cripple.

When I was in the eighth grade Grandma, my mother, and I all got boils. Mine were the worst. I had one on my knee and another worse one just above my belly button. It grew to the size of a purple plum and looked like one too. Dr. Ebeling took one look and decided to lance it then and there. First he gave me a shot , right into the boil, to kill the pain. It hurt like hell. I was very stoical or maybe just afraid to yell because it would upset my mother. Lancing the boil was not nearly so painful, but then Dr. Ebeling put a drain in the opening where all the pus had been. The drain amounted to a long string of gauze jammed into the farthest reaches. That also hurt like hell. He covered it all with a big gauze bandage about five inches square and an inch thick. It made my waist so big that I couldn't button my spring cotton skirts and had to wear a cardigan to cover up the big safety pins holding them up. Even with the cardigan the bulge was obvious, and I worried that my classmates would think I was pregnant.

Until after college, the Ebeling Clinic was the place I received medical attention, and every doctor, at almost every visit, said my tonsils should come out. Everyone my age had their tonsils out--it was the thing to do. My parents kept putting it off, partly because of the cost, but also because they both still had their tonsils and thought they must be there for some reason. Sometime in my thirties a different doctor looked in my throat and asked how old I was when my tonsils were removed. When I told him I still had them, he looked again and announced that he couldn't see them. By then routine tonsillectomies were a thing of the past. He explained that my tonsils had done their job when I was young and by now had atrophied to oblivion. I guess my parents were right.

A couple of blocks north of the Baptist Church, near the top of the viaduct and a few blocks down (west) from the high school, was the YMCA, site of the town's only swimming pool and of informal high school dances. The Y offered six free swimming lessons, over a two week period, to children age eight and over. During the summer between second and third grades I signed up, as did Nancy, Sharon, Annaly, and other kids my age. To prepare, I forced myself to learn to open my eyes under water, like a real swimmer. This involved filling the bathroom sink with water, sticking my face in, and screwing up the courage to open my eyes. By the time the lessons began I had mastered this skill.

On the first day, when we all lined up on each side of the small swimming pool, I recognized Mary Ellen Copner, who was a year behind me in school and only seven years old. I was furious that someone under eight was here when I was all of eight and a half and followed the rules like a good citizen; I wanted to tell someone, but then the teacher had everyone go to the shallow end, and I forgot about it. That first day, all we did was form a serpentine, jump around in the shallow end and splash water. During the second lesson, still in the shallow end, we learned how to kick while keeping our legs straight and holding onto the spit trough along the side of the pool. For the third lesson we had to kick while floating on our faces from the pool's side to the teacher several yards away. The fourth lesson began by standing at the side of the pool imitating the arm motions the teacher demonstrated, and then getting in the shallow end, bending over until our faces were in the water, and practicing the arm motions with feet firmly planted on the bottom. For the fifth lesson we put all this together, still in the shallow end, and swam from the side of the pool to the teacher standing half way across. We weren't shown how to turn our heads and breathe, which would come sometime in the future. The pool was narrow enough to swim across while holding your breath. The last lesson was graduation day. Those of us who had stuck it out lined up along the side of the pool, and one by one we swam across the deep end, feet kicking away, arms propelling madly. Everyone got across except for Mary Hantleman, who had perfect attendance in Sunday School but panicked half way across and grabbed the teacher who was swimming right beside her. When my turn came I took a deep breath, pushed off, and whaled away with my arms and legs, reaching the other side almost before I began.

A few days later when we went back to pick up our certificates three of us had been selected to have our picture taken for the newspaper! The other girl must have known ahead of time, because she had on a nice party dress, whereas I had on my usual jeans and T-shirt, as did the boy. We trooped down to the pool and posed with the teacher by the diving board. Thus I became a celebrity.

From then on I went to the Y regularly, honing my skills, though I didn't learn to dive until several years later following a series of painful belly-flops. The same summer that I learned to swim at the Y, Sharon's mother took Sharon, Nancy and myself to Clear Lake for a series of more swimming lessons, where we learned to dog-paddle. Therefore, I considered myself a veteran swimmer and happily showed off to cousin Margie at Big Lake when the Spokane relatives were in town. She took

113

me down a peg by pointing out that my right arm wasn't coming out of the water when I demonstrated the YMCA crawl.

P.E. was required in the first two years of high school, and each year the first activity in the fall was swimming. Being none the wiser, as a freshman I had first period P.E., so as soon as I got to school I had to deposit my books in my locker and trudge four blocks down the hill, carrying a bag containing my swim suit, swim cap(s) and nose plugs for a half hour of swimming before trudging back up the hill for second period. I was fourteen and fastidious with my appearance, so like most girls my age I put my hair up in pin curls each night and combed my hair out in the morning. With first period swimming, I could keep my scarf on until I got to the Y and not comb my hair until after swimming. I tried various combinations, including wearing two swim caps and using spoolies instead of bobby pins, to try keeping my hair dry. Only once was I successful, and when I repeated the method the next day my hair got soaked. Eventually the class finished the swimming unit and moved on to badminton in the gym, but I spent the first several weeks of high school with at least part of my hair wet and straggly. The next year I had P.E. fourth period, after lunch, so I only had to spend half a day looking like a creep.

The water tower and cemetery were just north of the high school. Each senior class traditionally and illegally painted their graduation year on the water tower. During our freshman year, however, some of my female classmates (who shall remain anonymous) dared to scale the tower and paint '59 over the '56. The seniors were furious, of course, which may be why some obnoxious senior girls disrupted the freshman class assembly. Within a day or two '56 was back on the water tower, where it remained for the rest of the year.

On special days such as Easter, Christmas, or Memorial Day (which Mom called Decoration Day) we took flowers to the cemetery. In the spring we took flowers from the yard (daffodils, bluebells, early roses, rhododendron blossoms), but in the winter, when flowers were scarce, Daddy made wreaths from evergreen trees and the holly bush on the south side of the house. I don't recall taking flowers to the graves of Daddy's family (Grandma Grimes and Howard, Daddy's brother who died before I was born), though I remember visiting the spot. I imagine Aunt Ruth took care of that. Mom always took a little spade to clean out the metal vases set in the ground by the graves. Her family's graves were all together under some big fir trees on the west side of the cemetery. Her father, my Grandpa Ward, was buried under half of a granite tombstone. The other half was waiting until Grandma died. Beside it was the grave of Barbara's mother, my Aunt Mary, who died before I was born. There was a small marker for Grandma's babies who had died, and a large tombstone for Grandma's parents (my great-grandparents), John and Margaret Knox, with the inscription, "Though lost from sight, in memory held dear." Grandma's sisters, my great-aunts Maggie and Siddie, were there too, later on, as was Aunt Claire, buried next to her sister Mary. My parents' ashes are buried on the graves of Grandma and Grandpa Ward. Someday mine will be buried next to them, on Barbara's mother's grave, the aunt I never knew.

From our house to Hillcrest Park, then down the hill to the business district, up the viaduct to the high school, and back to our house made a complete circle and comprised the town as I knew it, growing up.

THE COUNTRYSIDE AND BEYOND

"Out in the country" referred to anything beyond the city limits. Since farmland surrounded the town, naturally I was exposed to farm life to some degree. The richest farmland was on the Skagit delta, mainly west of town. My father's best friend was Phil Jennings who, until he married, lived in the family farmhouse between Mount Vernon and La Conner. Both Daddy and Phil were avid hikers and photographers and belonged to a camera club. Once or twice a year camera club members and their families gathered at the Jennings farmhouse. I spent my time playing with Phil's nieces, Martha and Linda Hart, both a bit younger than I but big, husky farm girls who always squeezed the breath out of me in their delight at having a girl to play with instead of their younger brothers. We played in their unheated upstairs hallway, racing from one end to the other and sliding down the stairs. One time I got a big sliver in my rear end from the stairs and went howling to my mother, who was in the dining room sitting next to Phil. She insisted on examining the damage right there and pulled down my pants while Phil made a remark about my cute bottom. I was embarrassed and furious with Mom, though she did remove the sliver. After that we sat on cushions while sliding down the stairs. Since these visits occurred in the evening, I had little exposure to the farm itself, though I do recall seeing the farm bull, a great beast with a ring in its nose.

After fourth grade I got a more thorough farm experience when my friend Elly's family bought a farm on the Britt Slough Road south of downtown. I loved visiting Elly on the farm. They didn't have horses, but Elly said maybe we could ride on one of the cows. Our favorite place to play was the big hay barn. In the fall it was piled almost to the rafters with big bales of hay. Using the bales as giant stair steps, we climbed mountains of hay. We found openings between bales and crawled inside along short tunnels, sometimes to a small cave. Once we found a nest of tiny kittens, so new their eyes were still closed.

As winter wore on, the cows ate more and more hay, and the mountains shrank. By spring, the hay held few enchantments. That's when we discovered the rope and pulley, used for hauling bales up to the side lofts and for making the mountains of hay in the center of the barn. The pulley slid along a track just below the high gable, from one end of the barn to the other. The rope, now that most of the hay was gone, hung

Elly and vegetable garden

all the way to the floor, and we found we could run with the rope and then swing, and the pulley would travel along the high beam carrying us from one end of the barn to the other. The bales were still high enough along one side for us to climb to the loft. We spent the morning swinging from loft to loft, from one side of the barn to the other, in great sailing arcs. It was like flying--the most fun we'd ever had.

At lunch in the big kitchen with Elly's parents and brothers, we could hardly wait to get back to the barn. We jabbered enthusiastically as we planned our afternoon--a mistake as it turned out. When he stood up from the table, Elly's father announced that there would be no more playing in the hay; it was far too dangerous. Then the crowning blow: after thinking it over, he had decided it wouldn't be a good idea to let us ride one of the cows. It might be harmful to the cow.

After eighth grade my by then best friend Patricia's family bought a farm on the Calhoun Road west of town, where they lived until after we finished high school. Of course, I spend a lot of time there, mainly staying overnight. Away from city lights, the stars were brighter than in town, and one August Patricia and I stayed up half the night watching the Perseid meteor shower. They bought a calf which they named Janet, after me. Then they bought another one, which they named Steve, after my unrequited love interest. Most of the time Patricia and I didn't spend much time together on the farm, because town had better things to do, such as attending high school games or other activities, going to movies, and shopping.

Starting around age ten most of my contemporaries who didn't already live on farms spent long summer days working in the strawberry, raspberry, spinach, and flower bulb fields. With all my friends slaving in the fields, I reluctantly joined them, earning precious little except, perhaps, gathering enough fodder for another book someday. Those summers convinced me I had better plan on going to college.

My family loved to go places, and since the town was small we didn't have to go far before we were out in the country. At least once a week we left town, almost always to do something outdoors, which I enjoyed. Some excursions were brief, such as a drive up Little Mountain, practically in our backyard, to climb the rickety wooden observation tower and look out over the valley. If the tide was in we could see the Swinomish Slough by La Conner, far to the west, and the Skagit River winding south of downtown, then splitting into the North and South Forks to form Fir Island. A slightly farther drive took us to Devil's Mountain, where trilliums bloomed in the spring and Mom filled a washtub with moist, rich decayed vegetation to supplement the soil in her flower beds. Big Rock, between Clear Lake and Big Lake, was also nearby. The first time I climbed it I was pretty small as shown in the picture Daddy took of Aunt Ruth, me, and Butch-dog looking at the view from the top.

On weekends we ventured farther, sometimes to shop in Bellingham or Seattle, or to see the animals at the Woodland Park zoo. The smell of "Monkey Island" was unforgettable. In the summer we picnicked on Whidbey Island or on a sand bar up the Skagit River beyond Sedro Woolley. Once we got there I enjoyed such excursions, but sometimes, usually when the weather discouraged outdoor activities, some adult might say, "Let's go for a ride." This meant driving around for an hour or two with no particular destination in mind, just looking out the windows, never getting out of the car. I hated going for rides, partly because I was bored, surrounded by adults, with nothing to do but listen to their talk; but I also hated it because I got carsick. Mom routinely packed bath towels to mop up after me if the driver (Daddy or an uncle) didn't stop in time. We might go to see the tulip fields in the spring, or down by Conway to look at recent flood damage, or around March's Point when it was still a beach, before oil refineries took it over, or to Bay View on the other side of Padilla Bay. Larry remembers a trip we took to Wenatchee when Uncle Del had to stop numerous times so I could throw up, walk a bit, and take deep breaths of fresh air. I asked, "Uncle Del, can't we just

118

<u>walk</u> to Wenatchee?" It helped if I could sit in the front seat and look at the road ahead, or if I could open a window slightly and stick my hand out. Even so, since all the men smoked the car reeked of cigarettes, and usually I was in the back seat, too short to see out the front window, fighting nausea and trying not to look out the side windows, a sure recipe for disaster.

Cow Pie Hill

Sometimes Mom and I went along when Daddy drove around taking pictures. These drives weren't too bad, because when he found a promising spot Mom and I got out and walked around while he set up the camera and took various shots. On one memorable occasion we stopped in an area northeast of town called the Nookachamps. While Daddy prepared to photograph an old barn on a hillside, I amused myself running up and down the hill--until I lost my footing and fell face first in a cow pie. Daddy got some good photos that day; a framed print of the hill and barn hangs on my wall today.

I thought I didn't get seasick. Roggie liked to fish, and sometimes he and Aunt Claire, my folks, the dogs (Timmy and Rusty) all went to Camano Island, hired a boat from a place called Camp Grande, trolled across to the east side of Whidbey Island, and dug clams. That was good, because I got to set foot on land, run around while the adults dug clams, and eat lunch before trolling back to Camano. Watching for cabin cruisers--the more portholes the better--entertained me. However, just going out fishing all day was BORING and hard to tolerate. One time we headed out the Swinomish Slough, intending to spend the day fishing in Skagit Bay, but Roggie slightly misjudged the tide, which was on its way out. We were left high and dry near Goat Island. To my delight we had to spend the day exploring the Island, waiting for the tide to come back in so we could go home.

Since I never got seasick during any of these boat trips, I thought I was immune. Then, as a young adult, I boarded a ship in Tyne Ports, England, and crossed the North Sea in 22 hours. It took ten hours for me to get seasick, and for the remainder of the journey I was flat on my back. As long as I didn't move, I was fine. When we entered calm waters approaching Bergen, Norway, I got up.

About forty years later I got seasick again, on a cruise from Florida through the Panama Canal. North of San Diego we hit eighteen-foot seas, and once more I was fine as long as I stayed horizontal. Confined to the stateroom, I spent the evening watching a movie on closed-circuit TV: *The Perfect Storm*, in which everyone drowns.

BIG LAKE

East of Mount Vernon, against the Cascade foothills, is a string of lakes: Clear Lake, Lake Cavanaugh, Lake McMurray, Lakes Ten and Sixteen, and the biggest of these, aptly named Big Lake. Grandpa bought a cabin on the west side of Big Lake in 1943. It was six miles from town and a dump, with covered porches along three sides, two rooms (kitchen and living/dining room), and an attic accessible via an outdoor stairway on the porch by the kitchen door.

Big Lake cabin, after side porch enclosed

My earliest memory of the cabin is running back and forth along that U-shaped porch with Ray Bloom. On summer weekends, if we didn't go on a picnic to Whidbey Island or up the River with Mom's side of the family, we usually went to Big Lake with Daddy's side. Upstairs in the attic were two or three lumpy double beds with carved headboards and footboards, cobwebs, and lots of dust. Double doors opened off the attic toward the lake. Downstairs was a remarkable fireplace with a floor-to-ceiling chimney and a white plaster-like finish, sculpted into swirls, peaks, and blobs like meringue. I remember standing in front of a roaring fire to warm up after a swim or a

120

cold boat ride. Once when I accidentally fell into the marshy creek that ran along the north side of the property, the fire dried me off in no time and steamed my legs as well. I had to keep turning in order not to get cooked.

Grandpa in the boat he made

Grandpa loved to fish, and so did his dog, Butch. Fishing poles, nets, and baskets hung along one side of the main room. Grandpa fished mainly for perch, which were bony and inedible. When he caught a fish Butch got so excited he sometimes fell into the lake, and once he got a fishhook caught in his lip. "Goddamn dumb dog," Grandpa said.

There was a wooden dock and a walkway of rough boards running from the dock to the cabin. Eventually this was replaced with a concrete sidewalk, reducing the hazard of getting slivers in bare feet--mainly my problem, because I kept forgetting not to slide my feet. I remember sitting on Uncle Del's lap while he dug out my slivers with his jackknife. Every time I opened my mouth to howl Mom popped in a spoonful of beans. "Have another mouthful of beans" became a family expression for "stop complaining."

One Labor Day weekend at Big Lake, when I was in high school, I went for a boat ride with Ruth and Del, and we passed a boat with people water skiing. We hung around to watch--water skiing was something new--and Del realized he knew the man operating the boat. Before long I was invited to give it a try, and after falling in a few times I got up on two skis and made a couple of circles before landing in the drink. Then Del tried, and he made it up too. That settled it. He spent the winter in his garage building a wooden boat big enough for hauling a water-skier. He painted it white with red trim and christened it "Larkay" after Larry and Kay. That was the beginning of family water skiing at Big Lake. I liked to let go of the tow rope at just the right time to ski up to the side of the dock so I could get out without getting my hair wet, and one memorable time I miscalculated and skied right up onto the dock. For some reason there were several large (big as a breadbox) rocks scattered about at the end of the dock, and I somersaulted out of the water-skis and made a graceless landing among them. Miraculously, I wasn't even scratched. Thanks to hay-fever, I never learned to ski on one ski. One weekend when I was in college I was determined to do it and kept falling in until my nose was completely plugged up. Gradually, with the help of a nasal spray, it cleared up, but then my sense of smell was gone. Though eventually it came back, I was afraid I might lose it permanently, as my father had, so I gave up trying to ski on one ski.

The cabin had no running water, so we had to bring big gallon glass jugs of water from home for drinking and cooking. Even after the men dug a well in the front yard, the well water wasn't safe to drink. I'm not sure what it was used for, but I know it was often my job to prime the pump whenever it hadn't been used for a while. We always referred to the outhouse as the "boathouse"--not euphemistically but because its key

had been labeled "boathouse" when Grandpa bought the place. Over the years the cabin was improved in phases, replacing two sides of the porch with a bedroom and a main room extension that included an indoor

stairway to the upstairs. Eventually Larry and his wife Carol acquired the property as a vacation home and added indoor plumbing. Despite these improvements, it was impossible to make a silk purse out of a sow's ear (to coin a phrase), and they bulldozed the old cabin. Today Larry and Carol live there in a lovely retirement home on what is now prime real estate.

VACATIONS

For at least a week every summer we took a vacation, mostly on the Olympic Peninsula with Aunt Claire and Uncle Roggie. A few times we camped in tents at Baker Lake and on Orcas Island. To get to the Peninsula we drove to Fort Casey on Whidbey Island, where we caught the Keystone ferry to Port Townsend. One thing about the ferry I hated: the whistle, whose sudden, loud blast made me jump out of my skin. I kept my fingers in my ears until that was over with and put them back in as we approached Port Townsend. Daddy took a picture of Mom, Aunt Claire, Roggie, and Rusty on the ferry's outside deck. Part of my pant leg is visible between Aunt Claire and Mom, behind whom I was sniveling, waiting for the loud blast. After that, vacation was fun. Usually we spent the first night at an "auto court" called Maple Grove, on Lake Sutherland. One morning Roggie and I went fishing there, and I caught my first fish. From there we drove along Lake Crescent and on to Sol Duc Hot Springs, where I learned to float on my back before I could swim, and Daddy took me into the deep end while I held tight around his neck. Being a skinny kid, I was always cold playing in lake water, so the hot

springs were bliss!

Our Peninsula vacation continued at La Push, part of the Quileute Indian reservation, on the Pacific Ocean. Mom, Aunt Claire and I put on our swim suits and

123

waded into the water, jumping and screaming when the waves crashed around us. Rusty had the time of his life until a big wave dragged him out to sea. When the next wave brought him back, Aunt Claire managed to grab him and got scratched up pretty good for her efforts. After that, Rusty never liked the water, despite being a spaniel. I got so cold jumping in the waves that one time I went up on the beach and rolled in the hot sand. I was not at all happy when Daddy made me go back to the water to wash it off. We had checked out and were all packed up ready to leave one morning when someone yelled that the smelt were running. Thousands of the fish were rolling in the waves, flopping on the beach, being pulled back out to sea. Of course, we ran down to watch, and pretty soon we were wading out fully clothed, grabbing fish and throwing them back on the sand. We all got soaked, but we got enough smelt to fill Roggie's ice chest, and the resort owners let us back into the cabin to change into not so clean but dry clothes.

Since Aunt Claire, Roggie, and Mom all liked to fish, at least one day was spent in a rented boat. During one vacation near Dungeness Roggie caught a 25-pound King Salmon, which was pretty exciting, but I was happy when he let Daddy and me out of the boat to walk on the long spit while the others continued to fish.

In the summer of 1950, after third grade, we spent part of our vacation with Roggie and Auntie Claire at Spirit Lake at the base of Mount Saint Helens, which blew up many years later. I had saved two dollars from my allowance in hopes of spending it on a horseback ride. Daddy didn't believe in making reservations--something might come up to keep us from going, and he liked to be spontaneous--so when we arrived at Harry Truman's Resort, which was later buried in volcanic ash when the mountain exploded in 1980, there were no vacancies. I was crushed, because a sign indicated that rental horses were available, and then a girl my age rode by on a horse. Lodging was available across the lake, however, at Harmony Falls Lodge. Access was by boat only, so we unloaded the car, put everything in the launch, and away we went.

I sat in the back by the inboard motor, with my imitation brown alligator zipper pocket book (containing two one-dollar bills) on my lap. Suddenly, when I wasn't paying attention, the pocket book slipped off my lap and, with a splat, disappeared into the open bilge water in front of me. I was devastated, assuming the bilge was open to the lake water below and envisioning my wallet, the two dollars, and all hope of riding a horse sinking into the murky depths. Doubtless there were tears, only slightly eased when Roggie explained that the bilge was a contained device. So what, I thought. My hopes still lay in the murky depths, irretrievable.

We hauled our stuff to the cabin, where Mom and Auntie Claire fixed our dinner. Later someone knocked on the door. There stood the boatman, holding up a greasy, smelly imitation alligator pocket-book. Inside, the two one-dollar bills were wet but intact. Mom clipped them

on Bucky at Dungeness--A

to the clothesline where they dried out by the time we left for the Olympic Peninsula and the second part of our vacation. There, I sulked and whined until Daddy asked around and found out about a girl with a horse near our cabin at Dungeness. He offered to pay to let me ride "Bucky," but the girl's mother refused the money, and so the girl and I rode the big, gentle retired work horse, for two days. I was terribly proud of my saddle sores. Before we caught the ferry for home, I spent the two dollars on a bronze horse statue I found in a Port Townsend store.

The next summer, when I was ten, Daddy did make reservations. We planned a vacation too good to be true. My parents and I were going to spend a week with Aunt Claire, Roggie, Barbara, Curtis and Danny, at the Double-T Ranch in British Columbia. It was near Bridge Lake, great for trout fishing, and the ranch had saddle horses for horse-crazy girls such as myself. We reserved a cabin big enough for the eight of us. Then Curtis was offered the job in Alaska, which he couldn't pass up, and shortly before the departure date the telephone operators went on strike. Aunt Claire, as chief operator, was considered "management" and had to stay home and work the switchboard until the strike was settled. Of course, Roggie stayed home with her, so instead of eight there were just five of us: my folks, myself, Barbara and Danny.

Auntie Claire had promised that she would match every quarter I saved. By the time August 1951 rolled around I had saved ten dollars, so I had twenty dollars in all, more than enough to rent a horse for a week at two dollars a day. I kept the money in a red plastic purse and attached a leftover piece of upholstery (Daddy had reupholstered the couch and matching chair the previous winter) to the zipper ring. I liked to fling the purse over my shoulder and swing it around my head, holding on to the upholstery strip. I wasn't taking any chances of repeating last summer's bilge water episode.

Mid-afternoon on our first day of travel we stopped for gas and to use the restrooms. Twenty miles farther down the road I realized my purse was missing. "Goddammit, Janet," Daddy said as he slowed to make a U-turn. Some women had been going into the rest room as we came out. The purse and the week of riding horses sank once again into the bilge of despair. As we pulled into the gas station the attendant came out to meet us, swinging the purse by the upholstery strip. Inside were my twenty dollars and a note from a 70-something woman, Mrs. Emma Pheasant from Tonasket, Washington.

When I got back home I wrote to her, thanking her and describing how I'd saved the money, and how I spent it. For several years we exchanged Christmas cards. One evening many years later the local news featured an Eastern Washington apple farmer who had recently built housing for migrant workers. He was Earl Pheasant from Tonasket--probably her son.

After that, it was a wonderful week. Mom and Barbara fished every day, while Daddy took lots of pictures and babysat Danny and me, when I wasn't riding a horse, which was most of the time. The first horse I got on was Smokey, who didn't go anywhere; he wouldn't budge no matter how hard I kicked his sides. So Daddy took a picture of Danny and me sitting on him. The following days I got one of the more lively horses-- Kitty or Diamond or Dealy--and the highlight of the week was the day I got to go with the other girls and Jack, the ranch hand, to

Danny and me on Smokey

round up the cattle. Our roundup amounted to riding through the woods with Jack until he found the cattle and herded them back to the ranch. I felt like a real cowgirl. For the most part, Daddy was able to control Danny, but one day he slipped through the corral fence and headed for the horses. What stopped him was a pile of manure which he stepped into up to his ankle. Poor Daddy had to clean him up, and after that

126

Danny was subdued for a short time. Basically I considered him a pest and brat, but I had to laugh when he pointed to some cows and asked, "Janet, are them cows or cattles?"

In the evening, after cleaning the catch of the day and storing it in the ice house, Barbara sometimes sat in the car listening to the Mount Vernon Milkmaids baseball game. Amazingly, way up there in Canada the car's radio got clear reception of Mount Vernon's radio station, KBRC. Because there were bears in the area, Barbara was uneasy sitting by herself in the car, so Daddy often accompanied her. She was also nervous about going to the outhouse, a few yards away from the cabin. Once when she was in there Daddy sneaked up and threw a big stick into the brush next to the outhouse. Barbara was quiet for a long time and finally asked, "Uncle Forrest, is that you?"

SEATTLE SHOPPING TRIPS

Until I was in high school, Interstate 5 was no more than an idea, and driving the sixty miles south to Seattle took two hours. Highway 99 ran through town as a two-lane street; passed through Marysville and Everett, with a string of stop lights; and negotiated an endless stretch of billboards, real estate office, motels (and older "auto courts"), restaurants, and gas stations—from Lynnwood to the city center. Two or three times a year, from age four or five until I graduated from high school, my family made all-day shopping trips. Recalled now, they form a series of impressions of a small-town girl's Saturday trips with her family to the big city.

We started early—my parents, Aunt Claire, Uncle Roggie, and myself. Daddy and Roggie sat in front, while I sat between my mother and Aunt Claire in the back. Sometimes Aunt Claire applied nail polish in the car, then splayed her fingers and shook them to dry. Until Marysville, we passed through rural countryside, chatting about plans for the day, watching for landmarks as we made our way south. One such landmark was the "Upside-Down Bridge" across the Snohomish River between Marysville and Everett. When I was quite small, we had taken a train trip to Seattle; viewed from the train trestle below the highway, to me the road bridge had seemed upside down. South of Everett the highway widened to four lanes as we began to get into the suburbs ("rhubarbs" in the family lexicon). Moving along wide Aurora Avenue, we passed the Evergreen/Washelli cemeteries with row upon row of white grave markers, the Twin T-Ps Restaurant, Green Lake, the Aqua Theater, and the pedestrian overpasses near Woodland Park. When we spotted the big globe, around which revolved the neon words, "It's in the P-I," we were almost downtown. Our usual parking lot was near the ultimate department store, Frederick and Nelson. Underneath the parking lot were public restrooms. I recall a white floor made of tiny octagonal tiles, and a restroom matron who was lame.

The streets bustled with Saturday shoppers, mostly still empty-handed and eager. I stared at a blind man sitting on the sidewalk, playing an accordion, and at clusters of black people, unfamiliar sights in my town. Since we had about an hour until lunchtime, we separated briefly from the men. With Mom and Aunt Claire, I waited for the "walk" sign and surged across the street as part of a human wave, met halfway by another wave coming toward us. We spent our time on the first floor of Frederick and Nelson looking at the counters of perfume, gloves, scarves, and handbags. The time before lunch was for looking and planning. Serious shopping was saved for the afternoon. If we had time, we might take the escalator up a flight or two. I loved escalators—something else Mount Vernon did not have—and gazed admiringly at the stylishly dressed manikins, with their long eyelashes and bright red lips, secretly wishing my mother and aunt looked like them.

For lunch we rejoined the men at Ben Paris' Restaurant, just down the block from Sherman Clay, where my father had gone to admire the Hammond organs he could not afford. Ben Paris' was down a long flight of wide stairs from street level, ending at a pool with live trout swimming and coins at the bottom. To the left was the sporting goods store, with guns, fishing tackle, camping equipment, and, mounted on the supporting pillars, trophy heads of moose, elk, deer, and other game animals. After lunch, Roggie would browse there for fishing tackle. To the right of the stairs was the restaurant, its wooden booths varnished dark brown. The menu listed something pleasing to each of us; for me, a hot turkey sandwich.

After lunch we separated again. When I was small I went along with my mother and aunt. First we headed for another restroom stop, this time the family lounge on Frederick and Nelson's sixth floor, taking a side trip through the alcove displaying Steuben glass. I could have lingered there for hours admiring the figures and landscapes etched in glass prisms and mounds, or molded figures such as a leaping trout on the verge of catching a bright gold insect—all displayed against dark blue velvet. In the family lounge, adjacent to the women's restroom, was a row of telephone booths and a number of telephone directories from cities all over the country. Once I looked up my hero, Guy Madison, in the Los Angeles directory, but without success. Probably his number was unlisted. When Sharon moved to Bellevue, I could call her for ten cents from one of those telephones. Almost as exciting as talking to Sharon was using the dial phone, which we didn't yet have at home.

128

Besides Frederick and Nelson, the afternoon shopping itinerary included The Bon Marche, Rhodes, and sometimes Penney's, Nordstrom's (which then was a high class shoe store), and Best's Apparel. If there was time, the women went to the Public Market. None of this appealed to me, especially the Market, which was smelly and confusing. I hated shopping and felt dragged along. One day, when Uncle Roggie had not come to Seattle, my father invited me to spend the afternoon with him.

Thus I gained entrance to a world infinitely more fascinating to me than that of my mother and aunt. The afternoon was there to enjoy by going, seeing, doing—not to use prudently for shopping. One time we went down to Ye Olde Curiosity Shoppe on the waterfront, where a stuffed mermaid—supposedly fished out of some distant sea—adorned one wall. We saw a passenger ship depart for the Orient, with people on board waving to those left behind on the pier, just like in the movies. Another time my father guided me along First Avenue, past bums and beggars, to the Smith Tower, the tallest building west of the Mississippi. We took the elevator to the Chinese Room on the top floor and watched the tiny cars and people below. While there we saw a what seemed to be a miniature fire engine, its siren faintly sounding, leave its stationhouse and wind its way through traffic.

If the weather was disagreeable we went to a movie. We saw *Mogambo, Pandora and the Flying Dutchman, Marty,* and *The Rose Tattoo*, all first-run films at big downtown theaters. Mount Vernon's two theaters showed only second-run films, sometimes almost a year after they were first released. The epitome of Seattle movies was *The Day the Earth Stood Still* at the Coliseum. It was one of the best of a series of 1950's science fiction films about extra-terrestrials. The huge theater's acoustics were so good, Daddy said later, that when the flying saucer landed he felt as if it were coming down on top of us. As much as I enjoyed that movie, I was even more impressed with the theater. Constructed during the heyday of filmmaking, it was a true movie palace—the gaudiest, largest, most extravagant theater I had ever seen. The walls were marble (or appeared to be); there were three balconies (neither of Mount Vernon's theaters had even one); and when the deep pink curtain rose, the bottom edge gathered into elegant scallops.

Emerging from movie wonderland in the late afternoon, we found the downtown streets had changed. Hurry was in the air, people rushing to catch buses, parking lots emptying. Now I noticed street vendors, some selling popcorn or unshelled hot roasted peanuts in paper bags. Newsboys hawked the evening edition. Once headlines ominously declared that President Eisenhower had suffered a heart attack.

When we rendezvoused with my mother and aunt near the candy counter in Frederick's, Aunt Claire was laden with purchases: new shoes, leather gloves, lacy undies, sometimes a new suit. She was a working woman and could justify such extravagance. Mom also had packages, most of which were quickly packed away in the car's trunk and forgotten until they reappeared as Christmas or birthday presents.

In the dusk, our car's interior lighted by neon signs and headlights, we joined the slow procession moving out of the city and chatted in spurts about the day's incidents. Viewed from the Aurora Bridge, the big "Grandma's Cookies" sign at the north end of Lake Union dominated the twinkling lights below. We drove north and then stopped for dinner somewhere along Aurora, maybe at King Oscar's Smorgasborg.

Driving on after dinner, my mother, with some rustling, produced several white paper bags containing various chocolates from Frederick and Nelson's candy counter. There were quarter-sized nonpareils, chocolate-covered raisins, peanut clusters, droplets with ridges that swirled to a peak. We chose two or three apiece; then the bags disappeared, saved for parties and holiday gatherings.

As we continued north, conversation dwindled. Lights flashed past less frequently. Thoughts turned inward, and the day's events began shaping themselves into stories to be told to family members awaiting us at home; later to be recalled among ourselves as family lore. North of Marysville, we pushed homeward in silent darkness, lulled by the engine's steady hum, our own thoughts, and the presence of each other.

VISITING SHARON

After the Petersons moved to Bellevue Sharon and I remained best friends and wrote to each other regularly. During the summer and school vacations we visited each other for days at a time. I would ride the Greyhound bus from Mount Vernon to Seattle, where Sharon met me, and together we took the suburban bus to Bellevue and then walked to her house. Sometimes there was quite a wait for the suburban bus, and once to pass the time I suggested we walk to Pioneer Square and go to the top of the Smith Tower, where Daddy had taken me recently. So we walked all the way from the Greyhound Station to the Smith Tower, about twenty city blocks, carrying my suitcase. At the time Pioneer Square was a slum, and we attracted quite a bit of unwanted attention. However, when we got to the Chinese Room at the top of the Tower the view was as thrilling as I remembered. We had enough sense never to tell our parents about this adventure.

Sharon's house was south of Bellevue's small downtown area, just a short walk to Lake Washington where we went swimming every day. Her brother, Lee, or an older neighbor girl came with us. Lee didn't swim; he thought the water was too cold, and so did I, but I had to do whatever Sharon did. After swimming we sometimes walked to town or visited whatever horses we could find in the neighborhood. During one summer visit Sharon, Lee, the neighbor girl, and I all slept in a tent in the backyard and told ghost stories. Here is a letter I wrote home when I was eleven, postmarked August 16, 1952:

Sharon and I were in pre-pubescent love and walked around holding hands or with our arms around each other. Besides "Babydoll," we called each other Sweetie Pie or Honey Dew until Mrs. Peterson pointed out that a honey dew was a melon, which struck us as hilarious and led to another term of endearment: Melon, and then--why not--Cantaloupe. From that grew an analogy. When we weren't sleeping in the tent we shared Sharon's double bed. If someone's legs invaded the other's space she was told, "Melon, dear, get your roots back on your own side of the dirt." Gales of laughter followed.

Twice during the summer, after sixth grade and again after seventh, I went with Sharon to Orcas Island in the San Juans for a week of "Christian Service Camp." As soon as we got on the ferry we had to explore everything. Leaning over the rail on an upper deck, we could see jellyfish in the water below. Suddenly a boy stuck his head out of a porthole on the lower car deck, probably looking at the same jellyfish, and I asked Sharon, "Do you think I could hit him if I spit?" Slim chance, but worth a try. I worked up a big wad, let fly and hit the target smack in the center of his jacket collar. We both fell down laughing. Later we saw the same boy on an upper deck, the spit still in place, and fell down laughing again.

At camp we slept in barracks with an adult supervisor who strictly enforced lights out. During the morning there were lessons, as boring as Sunday School, but after that, camp was fun. The lessons didn't "take," because we behaved like little devils, making fun of "Pig Face," a girl we

Sharon and me call each other baby-doll We go swimming every day Carolyn always comes in too.
Guess thats all.
Love
Janet
Be sure to say Hello to Grandma for me

Ching Sharons dog was a bad boy he followed us and got in the black-berrie thorns.
Last night both of Carolyns cats slept in the tent with me.

The End

didn't like, and playing cruel tricks such as putting a dead starfish in someone's bed. After lunch there was usually an organized hike. One day, instead, we were driven up Mount Constitution and climbed the stone observation tower for the view of the San Juan Islands, Whidbey Island, and the mainland to the east. Sharon and I decided to run from there all the way back to camp. That was one time I couldn't keep up with Sharon, who made it all the way running, whereas I pooped out and walked the last half-mile or so. We went swimming in a nearby lake every afternoon before dinner. For some religious reason we could wear swimsuits but not shorts. After dinner we returned to the lake for a bonfire and a sing-along. I loved the songs: "Give me oil in my lamp...," "I've got a home in glory land...," "Halelu, Hallelu, Hallelu, Hallelujah! Praise ye the Lord," and others I've forgotten. During the last song, before the prayer, anyone so moved "went forward" to take Jesus as his or her personal savior. I failed to be so moved.

The last morning, before getting on the ferry, the entire camp went down to the lake again, where those who had gone forward during the week were fully dunked and thus born again. That was the end of camp, but I had gotten to spend a whole week with Sharon.

BELLINGHAM DENTIST

Except for getting carsick, almost all of my adventures out of town were positive experiences. However, one excursion we took repeatedly was most definitely NOT fun: going to the dentist in Bellingham. When I still had baby teeth Mom took me to Dr. Gervin in Mount Vernon for

133

the first time. He poked around in my mouth a bit; then I got down from the chair and watched while Mom had a tooth filled. Unfortunately Dr. Gervin died soon after that. The War had just ended and there was a shortage of dentists in town. Dr. Finley had bought Dr. Gervin's practice, but somehow our family's records had been lost, and Dr. Finley wasn't taking new patients, nor was any other local dentist, so when my new permanent teeth began to come in we had no dentist. I didn't see a dentist again until I was about nine years old. By then Barbara had married Curtis and lived in Bellingham, where she was able to get Mom and me an appointment with her dentist, Dr. Hunt. So began the ordeal.

I had major cavities in all my molars and some bicuspids. Filling them required several appointments, which meant I had to miss a half day of school and Daddy had to miss a half day of work to free up the car for the 25 mile drive to Bellingham. I had butterflies in my stomach from the time we left home until Dr. Hunt lowered the

Bellingham Bank Building

chair at the end of the appointment. If we had time I asked Daddy to go via Chukanut Drive, a scenic, twisting road above the water, rather than Highway 99, because it took longer and thus postponed the inevitable. I tried very hard not to get carsick.

Dr. Hunt's office was downtown in the Bellingham Bank Building. Typically, we arrived at one or one-thirty, the first appointment of the afternoon. Sometimes the door from the waiting room to the work area was closed, and hanging on the door knob was a sign reading, "The doctor will return at...," and beneath that was a clock face with hands set to the time of our appointment. The closed door was a relief, for it meant a short reprieve.

Soon, though, Dr. Hunt's wife, his assistant, opened the door and I marched into the torture chamber. As Dr. Hunt raised the chair I got a clear view of the shops along Holly Street below and of a distant church spire. Initially Dr. Hunt asked if I wanted Novocain. I said no--partly because I wasn't fond of needles, partly because I was in my tomboy phase, which required enduring pain tearlessly and soundlessly like Roy Rogers. Butterflies filled my chest and stomach as Dr. Hunt pulled the

134

instrument tray into place and raised the drill.

This was not the fast drill which is used today, but a slow, tedious instrument. Drilling away the decay, then drilling tiny tunnels to anchor the filling, could take a half hour to forty-five minutes. As the drill probed deeper into the tooth it got closer to the nerve, causing increasing pain as it moved round and round. Periodically Mrs. Hunt rinsed my mouth and directed me to spit into the little sink beside me. Then she shot air into the tooth , giving the nerve another jolt.

When Mrs. Hunt began to prepare the amalgam the worst was over. Tamping down the filling, scraping away the excess, and polishing it were like dessert after a bad meal. The butterflies were gone. As Dr. Hunt lowered the chair, the distant church spire and the shops along Holly Street disappeared from view. I was free--until the next appointment.

Once these major cavities were treated, I only had to see Dr. Hunt every six months. In those days, before fluoride treatments, I usually developed a cavity or two in the interval between visits. The drive to Bellingham, the butterflies, the chair, the drill, and the agony occurred regularly over the next few years until Dr. Hunt retired. By then Dr. Finley in Mount Vernon was accepting new patients. The first time he filled a tooth he asked if I used Novocain. Yes! I answered.

CULTURE

THE MOVIES

Cultural opportunities in Mount Vernon were pretty limited while I was growing up. Besides the two, sometimes three movie theaters, there were public high school performances such as plays and talent contests. My parents took me to movies fairly often even before I was in school, and when I got bored I said I had to "wee-wee." After my third trip to the restroom Mom told me I couldn't go to any more movies until I could sit through them. One early movie featured a woman who loved a man but stabbed him for some reason, and at the end there was a volcano in the background. In high school I read a library book called *Captain from Castile*, about a Spaniard who becomes a Conquistador, goes to Mexico, and is followed there by a girl who loves him. When I was in college I went home with a friend for the weekend, and one evening we turned on the TV in the middle of a movie. It was a love scene, and suddenly I realized the movie we were watching was the movie I remembered from childhood and that it was based on the book I had read in high school. What a moment of epiphany!

Most of the early movies I saw were Walt Disney features such as *Song of the South* or *Snow White*, or others made especially for children; and musicals starring Judy Garland, June Haver, or Jane Powell. Saturday double-feature matinees cost fifteen cents and often included a

Roy Rogers or Gene Autry movie. Roy's movies were in color, but Gene's were sepia, and at one of his movies I had a painful experience. Before the show started I stuck my feet between the back and cushion of the empty seat in front of me. Then a kid came along and sat in that seat, but I didn't get one foot out in time. The kid kept pushing on the seat, trying to get it all the way down, which he couldn't because my toe was there, getting crushed. Like Roy Rogers and Gene Autry, I stoically endured pain without a whimper. Finally the kid stood up and looked to see what was wrong with the seat, and I quickly yanked my foot out. Later the big toenail turned just the color of Gene Autry's movies--sepia. I called it my Gene Autry toe and wore it like a badge of courage as I ran around barefoot all summer.

When I was nine or ten a drive-in theater opened north of town. Our family didn't go there very often, but the science fiction thriller *The Thing* is memorable partly because of what happened before the movie began. Curtis was working in Alaska that summer, and Barbara and Danny came down for the day. In the evening they, my parents, myself and Grandma all piled into the car. When we got to the drive-in it wasn't dark enough for the movie to start, so Danny went to the playground just below the big screen, and eventually I was sent to get him. As I ran toward the screen I noticed a cute little boy waving at me from the back seat of a car. I trotted over to say hi and unknowingly ran between the car and the pole where the speaker was connected. The driver had already attached the speaker to the car's window, and the cord caught me at the neck and flung me flat on my back. knocking the wind out of me. I lay there gasping until I finally had a voice and said, "Oh, excuse me," got up, and continued on my journey to fetch Danny. When we got back

Ready to see yet another movie with Annaly

to the car I described the incident, once again causing Barbara to laugh so hard she almost wet her pants.

In junior high and high school movies were standard fare. Usually I went with a friend, often Annaly. The first movie I saw with Guy Madison in it was a 3-D western, *The Charge at Feather River.* That was before I developed a crush on him, so the thrill was not seeing Guy on the big screen but rather all those Indian arrows coming at you. Once Guy became my idol, I saw every new film he made: *The Command, On the Threshold of Space, The Beast from 20,000 Fathoms, Hilda Crane, Five Against the House,* and *The Last Frontier* (also starring Victor Mature, whom Sharon and I called Bawl Bag because he cried in *Demitrius and the Gladiators*; and Felicia Farr, who later married Jack Lemmon). I also saw every Debbie Reynolds and Grace Kelly movie, and every one with Tony Curtis and/or Janet Leigh, because Annaly was nuts about them, and just about every other movie that wasn't strictly for children.

LITERATURE

Though my college major was literature, and I went on to earn a Master's Degree in that subject, my literary adventures got off to a questionable start. One Christmas my cousin Larry gave me a subscription to *Loony Tunes,* which featured Porky Pig, Bugs Bunny and my favorite character, Mary Jane, who had a mouse friend, Sniffles. Mary Jane could say a magic phrase and become as small as Sniffles. Then the two of them went off on various adventures such as riding around in the sky with the Cloud People. My favorite comic book was *Little Lulu*, which I read whenever I could find it, even after college. After my second grade teacher took the class to the public library I was an occasional patron. The library, such as it was, consisted of a single room at one end of the city hall. At the other end was the fire station. I was not a voracious reader of books as was Annaly, who always had seven or eight library books at home and kept forgetting to return them on time, to the point where her father took away her library card. After that she used my card.

Oh, I had books at home, gifts from family members, favorites which I read more than once: a picture book by Margaret Wise Brown called *Baby Animals,* which Daddy brought me when he went to a Carpenters convention out of town; *Heidi* by Joanna Spyri from Barbara,

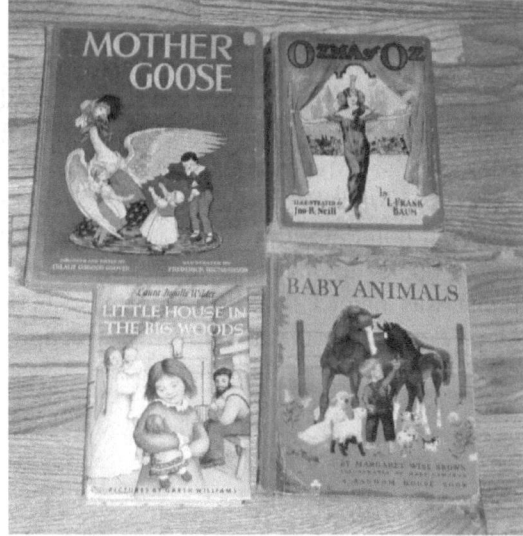

a book Grandma thought was too old for me, but I loved it; L. Frank Baum's Oz books from my mother, who had loved them as a child; *Little House in the Big Woods*, and *Once There Was a King*, from Aunt Carol. I still have these but have lost a picture book I still long for and whose title page I would recognize if I saw it.

Other than these, I read so few books as a

139

pre-teen that I still remember most of them. There was a paperback I found at June's Grocery, *Hobby Horse Hill* by Lavinia R. Davis, about a prissy girl who comes down off her high-horse while learning to ride a real horse with her roughneck cousins. At the public library I borrowed and devoured the rest of the "little house" books and a couple of books by Enid Blyton, whose name I recently learned by googling the titles: *The Castle of Adventure* and *The Valley of Adventure.* In grade school periodically teachers took the class upstairs to the school library, which, for want of a classroom, was housed behind the curtain on the auditorium stage. There I discovered *Candy* by Robb White, about a Florida girl with a sailboat, a blind boy, and an eye surgeon who restores his sight; *Cowgirl Kate,* about which I recall nothing, and another in the same series, *Cowboys and Cattle Drives*, whose main character grows up to be a Congressman from Texas. I've never been able to discover the title of another book about Texas featuring a tomboy named Francie Lou, who lived on a ranch near San Antonio.

When I was thirty-two and went to library school during a sabbatical, I had two goals: to get out of teaching freshman English, which involved endless reading of badly written 500-word themes; and to read all the great children's literature I had missed out on as a child. It was wonderful! I never read a Nancy Drew or Bobbsey Twins book, which, I learned in library school, were products of the Stratemeyer syndicate, ghost written by various unknown authors under the name Carolyn Keene, for example. Annaly ate these up, and as we grew older (junior high age) we shared an interest in some adult books such as *Gone with the Wind*, which we each read multiple times (after seeing the movie, which was re-released when we were in eighth grade) and always disagreed on whether or not Scarlett would get Rhett back. I thought no, she deserved to suffer, whereas Annaly thought yes, because Scarlett was a woman with womanly wiles. We also read everything Betty MacDonald wrote, beginning with *The Egg and I.* One summer afternoon at Annaly's we discovered in the bookcase a novel by northwest writer Patricia Campbell: *Lush Valley.* A better title, at least from our point of view, would have been "Lust Valley." I never read the whole book--just the rape scene, which occurred in a church pew (the rapist was named "Shully)," and a seduction scene later in the book. Until *Peyton Place* was published a couple of years later, that was the closest I came to X-rated literature.

So, while I read only a few good books during my grade school years, I was a voracious reader of movie magazines. To this day I remain a walking encyclopedia of Hollywood trivia published between 1949 and say 1955. It began in third grade when *Life* or *Look* came out with

an article on Shirley Temple's divorce. Auntie Ruth had a copy of the magazine, which caught my attention because of an article about a "blue baby" who had been cured by a new kind of surgery, the same that Alice Bolster would soon have. After reading the blue baby article I discovered the one about Shirley Temple. A few days later I saw her photo on the cover of *Modern Screen* and bought the magazine with my allowance. Some of the people it featured I had seen in movies, and it dawned on me that they were real people. My cousin Barbara bought movie magazines, and she began passing them on to me. A fan was born!

I read the gossip columns by Louella Parsons, Hedda Hopper, and Sheilah Grahame, and the feature articles about my favorite stars: June Haver, Jane Powell, Esther Williams, Janet Leigh and Tony Curtis. In my mind's eye I still see a color portrait of a starlet named Sally Forrest, someone I never heard of again. Movie stars went to night clubs (one article was entitled "We Swam our Way to Ciro's"), got divorces, had lots of clothes, lived in big houses in Beverly Hills, and smoked. They ate something called h'ors d'ouvres, which later on Annaly called "whore's ovaries." My vocabulary increased impressively:

"What's a miscarriage?" I asked Daddy.

"Why?" he responded, startled.

"Lana Turner had one."

I learned about talent scouts and hoped one would spot me. At school recess I played on the monkey bars and got pretty good at it, comparing myself to Debbie Reynolds in *I Love Melvin,* also starring Donald O'Conner.

When I bought a magazine entitled *Who's Who in Hollywood* I discovered a gold mine. It was filled with brief biographies of virtually every person who ever appeared on screen, a treasure chest of trivia: Cyd Charisse was born Tula Ellis Finklea; Cary Grant was Archibald Leach; Judy Garland was Frances Gumm, etc. Ida Lupino "never missed a paycheck." Janet Leigh (Jeannette Morrison) was married twice before wedding Tony Curtis (Bernard Schwartz)! Lana Turner (Julia Jean Mildred Frances Turner) had RH negative blood.

Barbara was visiting when I discovered a funny name for someone in the "music" category: "Listen to this guy's name," I laughed--"Hoggy Commercial." Barbara looked at the name and began to cackle; it was

Guy Madison as Wild Bill Hickok

Hoagy Carmichael, composer of "Stardust."

Guy Madison (Robert Moseley) was a transition idol from Roy Rogers (Leonard Slye) to real boys; he played Wild Bill Hickok on TV but also was hyped as a heart-throb. When new magazine issues came out at the first of the month I hit the newsstands searching for articles about Guy. I kept a scrapbook in which I pasted each article. My favorite was entitled "I

Believe," part of a *Photoplay* series, "How Stars Found Faith." Guy, I learned, was a man of character worthy of adoration, far superior to, say, Tony Curtis, who was merely handsome, or Annaly's idol, Eddie Fisher (Edwin Jack Fisher), who looked like a kid. Even so, when she got a reply to a fan letter we were both thrilled. The signature seemed to be real blue ink (fountain pen--ball points were rare), and just to be sure she wet her finger and smudged the ink. She took it to school to demonstrate and by the end of the day the signature was just a light blue smear.

By high school my interest in Hollywood began to wane. When I tried out for a high school play I discovered I had a bad case of stage fright, so there went my dreams of stardom. Guy Madison had eloped (after a quickie Mexican divorce from Gail Russell) with someone named Sheila Connolly, and six months later they had a baby girl, Bridget. Louella Parsons wrote, "Bridget, of course, was premature," but I suspected my hero had feet of clay. I lowered my sights to that cute sophomore in my algebra class, turned out for GAA (Girls' Athletic Association) to earn a letter sweater, and struggled with Spanish. In social studies, when we had to choose a career to research, I decided I wanted to be a stewardess.

DRAWING

From an early age I loved to draw with pencils and crayons. For my birthday one time I got a set of colored pencils. The blue pencil got used up first, because I learned that if I dipped it in water the lines resembled those of a fountain pen. Before I learned cursive I filled pages with squiggly lines which looked to me like real handwriting. Eventually I got my own fountain pen and bottles of various colored ink. I drew house plans and pictures of everything else, especially horses or glamorous women in fancy dresses. For the third grade Christmas poster contest I copied a picture from an old Christmas card: a cherub standing on an evergreen bough, lighting a candle. I was sure to win; everyone knew I was the best "artist" in the room. But Jimmy Myers, a poor student, drew a picture of a church which won the prize. What a blow!

A portion of the 3rd grade poster that didn't win

The next year I vowed to win. Daddy suggested a simple snow scene using just blue crayon on white paper, a single tree, and a house on a hill with smoke coming out of the chimney. Though I won the prize (a jigsaw puzzle and an umbrella), I didn't feel I had earned it, since it was Daddy's idea, not mine.

In fifth grade, drawing was my salvation. The teacher was Mr. Janes, who wasn't hired until late in the summer--obviously the best the school board could do, which wasn't much. It was his first year of teaching, having been in the War and then gone to college on the GI bill. Later I learned that he had hoped to teach high school shop but had to settle for us. We were a shattered class--at least I was shattered. At the end of fourth grade my best friends, the neighborhood gang, had all moved away, leaving nobody for me to pal around with. The girls at the top of the class pecking order were Connie, Jody, Jean and Jean. At the bottom were Ida, another Jean, and a drip whose name I've forgotten. Annaly, like myself, was somewhere in the middle, but she didn't care for horses and was too fat to run or climb trees.

Enter Mr. Janes, who had no clue what to do with thirty fifth graders. I think the only thing I learned in fifth grade was arithmetic: fractions, decimals and percentages. In a letter to Nancy I complained about how little we were learning. It went something like this: We're only 1/5 into our language book, 1/3 into the science book, 1/4 into the social studies book, etc. It was no secret that Mr. Janes had a favorite: Connie, who wasn't a particularly good student but was cute and had cute clothes and a cute personality. Mr. Janes was totally smitten.

Even Connie, however, didn't escape Mr. Janes' discipline, which included standing in the corner. Sometimes he ran out of corners and had students line up between corners facing the wall. When these measures lost their effect he brought out the blackboard torture for the boys, who naturally were the worst trouble makers. Mr. Janes would draw three circles on the board--one for each index finger, as high as the boy could reach, and one for his nose while standing on tiptoe. The boys had to keep their fingers and noses in the circles until Mr. Janes said they could sit down. Often their legs trembled as they struggled not to slip out of the circles. At least once all the corners were occupied, two or three students faced each side wall, and boys on tiptoe filled both front and back blackboards. When Annaly was sent to the corner and Ray Bloom to the blackboard, I knew something was wrong with Mr. Janes, not with Annaly or Ray. I was almost ashamed that only one other girl, the drip whose name I've forgotten, and myself were never sent to the corner.

Annaly never forgave Mr. Janes for causing her to miss a word on a spelling test. He had grown up in New Mexico and pronounced some words with a drawl. In this case the word was "everybody," which he pronounced "ever-body," and that's how Annaly spelled it. Of course, if she had studied the spelling list she would have known how to spell it, but Annaly was not used to studying. As an adult she told me she assumed that anything she didn't already know either wasn't true or wasn't important.

On my report card Mr. Janes wrote: "Janet likes to spend her free time making pictures." I drew and drew and drew--at least one drawing every day. Once a drawing was finished I lost interest in it and gave it away, usually to Jody, my biggest fan. When I went to her house to play after school one time, I saw that my drawings covered the walls of her small bedroom.

Evidently the school board heard from more than a few parents, because Mr. Janes didn't return the next year. My sixth grade teacher, Mr. Clark, was a nice man and good teacher, though I didn't fully recover from Mr. Janes and the loss of my four best friends for another year. In sixth grade I lost interest in drawing, except for horses. Sandy Bidwell was in Mr. Clark's room, and she liked to make cartoon-like drawings of her classmates. She joined my Campfire group and took the name "O-wa," meaning "to draw or paint." That was the name I had wanted, but Sandy spoke up first. I settled for "Ta-Wan-Ka," meaning "willing to undertake or attempt." What I had in mind was my physical derring-do, climbing trees or playing on the monkey-bars.

DANCING LESSONS

When I was five my mother signed me up for dancing lessons. The teacher was Miss Karen Irvin who later became a well known instructor at Seattle's Cornish College of the Arts. With her piano accompanist, Mrs. Rogers, Miss Irvin came on the train from Seattle once a week and gave dancing lessons all afternoon. They stayed at the President Hotel, and the next day they took the bus to Sedro-Woolley where they gave more lessons before returning to Seattle.

The lessons were held in a big room of the Episcopal Church downtown. While the mothers sat in chairs along one wall, the class had its lesson. That first year my classmates included Kathleen and Patsy Murphy, Ann Equals, and Barbara Dean, all of whom later went to high school with me. We worked at the barre, going through the positions (first, second, fourth and fifth--I never knew why we skipped third); and we learned steps: plie, changement, arabesque. We learned to arch our backs and kick the backs of our heads while holding on to the barre. When we got out of line Miss Irvin used psychology: "Girls! Pay attention. The Sedro-Woolley girls don't behave like that!" Halfway through the lesson we had a short break, and Miss Irvin chain-smoked Pall Malls. They were longer

Storybook doll costume

147

than regular cigarettes and very elegant in a Mrs. Flinnigan sort of way.

I took ballet lessons for two years and yearned to take tap dancing, which was featured big in movies such as *Look for the Silver Lining*, with June Haver and Ray Bolger (who also played the scarecrow in *The Wizard of Oz*). But Mom said she couldn't afford both and thought ballet was more important. For our recital in May our class members were dressed as storybook dolls. My costume was a blue gown with big white bows on the skirt. When the curtain went up, there was Mrs. Cannon with Lonnie Varnadore in the front row, just as they had promised.

By the second year I was in a class with mostly older girls, because Miss Irvin thought I had talent. We got pink toe shoes which we stuffed with soft lamb's wool that made our feet sweat. Miss Irvin expected us to practice at home. I didn't understand the concept and thought that either I could do it or I couldn't. Apparently most of the other girls felt the same and one day, out of patience, Miss Irvin questioned each of us as to why we hadn't practiced. "I don't have time," was the most frequent response, which is what I said when my turn came. Mom, who was watching, sagged in disgust.

Nevertheless, for the recital in the high school auditorium, she sewed me a pink tutu and a peasant costume for the two dances I was in. The recital combined the ballet classes from both Mount Vernon and Sedro-Woolley, so there were lots of little girls and a few boys running around the halls of the high school. We got ready in a classroom, and I got to wear lipstick and rouge on my cheeks. A week later there was another recital in Sedro-Woolley, but I missed it because I had injured my ankle while skipping rope and trying to cross the street at the same time, an accident I blamed on Annaly, who was half a block behind me.

That was the end of my dancing career. Mom said if I wouldn't practice she wasn't going to pay for lessons. That was fine with me, but a couple of years later, when I wanted piano lessons, I had a hard time convincing her I would practice.

PIANO LESSONS

We did not have a piano, and I wanted one. I wanted piano lessons to go with it. Several girls in my third grade class were starting piano lessons. That, along with joining Blue Birds (a warm-up for Campfire Girls), was what third grade girls did. I imagined myself a talented concert pianist, sweeping down the aisle in a purple (my favorite color) evening gown amid crashing applause from admiring throngs. The setting for this imaginary performance was the high school auditorium-- the closest thing in my experience to a concert hall. I pleaded sulked, argued and bawled for a piano.

Finally, my parents conceded that perhaps I was a budding genius, that their frugality might indeed by thwarting a great talent. Perhaps they owed the world.... My mother took me with her to the bank, where she soberly withdrew $200 in savings bonds from the safe deposit box. At the same time, I became vaguely conscious of an unfamiliar weight settling about my shoulders.

From the bank we went directly to MacDougall's Department Store and bought a new spinet piano, brand name Sterling, exactly the piano I had been hoping for, with plastic "ivories" and real wood finish. I had been afraid Mom might buy the old-fashioned, used upright we had also looked at. Such a piano would not at all have fitted into my picture. This impressive piece of furniture was really ours--mine!

A few days later, delivery men pushed the piano straight through the front porch arch and into the living room, where they set it against the wall opposite the windows. I danced around ecstatically. This was just what I had pictured. Mom's face was serious; those had been her savings bonds. Daddy said, "Well, I don't know. Maybe she'll prove me wrong." He still was afraid I would not practice once the novelty wore off, as it had with my dancing lessons.

My piano teacher was Mrs. Butler, whose baby grand piano filled the living room of her tiny house. Above the keys, where on my piano was written the word, "Sterling," hers said, "Chickering." The lessons were easy. I already knew where middle C was. I was supposed to practice half an hour a day, but in the beginning the lessons were so easy that ten minutes was enough. However, I wanted to be able to play like Cora Vandenberg, an eighth-grader whose lesson came after mine. Sometimes Cora warmed up before her lesson actually began, while I got on my coat and Mrs. Butler scolded her Pekingese dog, who was not allowed on the living room rug and did an excited toenail tap dance on the hardwood floor in the hallway. Cora's hands flew effortlessly over the keys. Her sheet music was black with notes, whereas mine was mainly white.

That Christmas I received two piano-related presents: a piano bench, which was marvelous, for it completed the effect of the piano's prominence in our living room; and an imitation leather briefcase for my music, with my full name, Janet Ann Grimes, stamped in gold letters. I loathed it on sight. Mrs. Flinnigan would not touch such a thing, nor did third grade girls go around with their names stamped on their possessions, and certainly not their middle names! The weight around my shoulders settled in for a long ride.

The weekly walk of less than a mile to my piano lesson after school became an ordeal. Since I lived only a block from school, rather than taking my albatross of a briefcase to school and going directly to Mrs. Butler's, I would run home to get it after school. That accomplished two things: first, I did not have to take the briefcase to school where classmates would see it; and second, classmates who walked home on the route I took to Mrs. Butler's would be a few minutes ahead of me. Just in case, though, I turned toward me the side of the briefcase where the gold letters spelled out my name. Once I reached the railroad tracks at the bottom of the hill I could relax. By then there was little chance of happening upon a classmate.

As the years went by, I began to dread the lessons more than the walk. Clearly I was not a prodigy. I was not even going to be another Cora. Grandma, who was living with us by then, noted to friends and family that I had become a clock watcher, referring to my practice sessions. One thing saved me from totally hating to practice: Mrs. Butler's wise suggestion that I reward myself during the last ten minutes of practice by playing something of my own choice. She suggested getting an old hymn book, but I had a better idea. In the piano bench was a dog-eared copy of *Songs the Whole World Sings*, which Daddy had picked up at a used book store. (While I was sweating over John

Thompson's books and Hannon drills, he taught himself to play by applying what he learned from my books to music he had played on his organ. So for the first time I played music familiar to me: "Grandfather's Clock," "Listen to the Mocking Bird," "Red River Valley," etc. That was fun. But still I watched the clock. Minute by minute, the years passed.

In eighth grade--my sixth year of penance--I tried out for Triple Trio, a singing group made up of nine eighth grade girls plus a piano accompanist. Triple Trio provided entertainment for local meetings of various adult groups. Being in Triple Trio was equivalent to being a cheer leader, which I did manage because I could do cartwheels and flips. I tried out as a singer, not as accompanist, which had little if any status. However, in order to have piano accompaniment while I and two friends tried out together, I played as well as sang. While I plinked away, we sang "Let the Rest of the World Go By" and "Tip-toe Through the Tulips."

Along with numerous other popular songs of bygone days, for years I had been playing these two songs during the last ten minutes of my daily piano practice. I had them down pat. Unfortunately, nobody tried out as accompanist for Triple Trio, and to my horror I was appointed. As a result, I was expected routinely to polish off three or four new pieces every couple of weeks. Accompanying requires the accompanist to keep up with the singers; you can't slow the tempo in order to let your fingers find the right notes. The singers keep on going, and if you do not keep up you have to read ahead and try to intercept them. Triple Trio's final performance for the year was for a group of adults meeting at the Campfire Lodge. Because the piano had no music stand and no flat place to lay the music where I could see it, I had to prop it open on a little ledge above the keyboard, where it kept collapsing, sometimes falling on the floor, while Triple Trio sang on, casting sympathetic glances my way as I scrambled for the notes and pages. Mercifully, that was the end of my playing the piano in public except for my final recital and playing background music at the school's annual Mother's Tea in the cafeteria. The tea was not too bad. It was too noisy for anyone to hear my mistakes.

Recitals were unhappy affairs from the beginning. At my final recital I was the oldest of Mrs. Butler's pupils, and theoretically the most advanced. I sat in Mrs. Butler's dining room listening to all the other students perform ahead of me. I followed Carolyn Sande, two or three years younger than I, and clearly gifted. (Like Cora Vandenberg, she went on to take organ lessons.) Now, like Cora at my first recital, I played last. But unlike Cora, I did not play with a flourish. I played with my usual frozen fingers and dragged my sheet music with me, because I hadn't memorized it. At least this time it did not fall on the floor.

I was relieved that this was my last recital. High school provided a convenient excuse. I argued that I would have so much homework that I wouldn't have time to practice. This was not true, but my parents apparently felt that six years of penance was enough. The weight lifted from my shoulders, and in its place was a gram of humility.

My piano playing would have ended with this whimper had it not been for the ten minutes of pleasure incorporated into my practice sessions, which showed me that playing the piano could be fun. As an adult, on visits home, I often sat at the old Sterling for over an hour, playing voluntarily. Maybe the $200 in savings bonds, the lessons, and the hours of practice were time and money well spent after all.

THE VIOLIN

There was a time when I simply <u>had</u> to have a violin. What may have precipitated this was a Judy Garland/Van Johnson movie, *In the Good Old Summertime*, circa 1949. A supporting role featured a beautiful, glamorous young woman violinist who entered a contest to study music in Europe. For the time being, the image of her standing on the stage in a lovely gown, playing beautiful music on a borrowed Stradivarius, supplanted my mental picture of the glamorous concert pianist. I <u>knew</u> I was destined to play the violin and was so insistent, so persuasive, that even my father began to weaken.

Fortunately he couldn't afford to buy me a violin, so he decided to make a "pretend" one--a cigar box violin--to see if that would satisfy me. He went to work in the basement and really did start out with a cigar box, but that was just the beginning. He took it apart and carved the lid and bottom to resemble the shape of a violin, even carving little "S" shaped openings like those in a real violin; he made a neck from a stick of wood, and attached the top and bottom to it. Next he inserted little wooden wedges in several places between the top and bottom sides to keep them apart. To enclose the two pieces, he glued a thin strip of cardboard, about an inch wide, all around the edges

153

between the top and bottom. Then he sprayed the entire creation with shiny silver paint. When that dried, he added the final touch, some broken guitar strings he had saved, which he attached at the top end of the neck and just below the curved openings on the top side.

Now all I needed was a bow, easily fashioned from an extra long, thin piece of kindling and a length of string from the big ball of it Mom kept in a kitchen drawer. Voila! I happily sawed away, delighted with my violin, imagining myself as the glamorous violinist in the beautiful gown. It was the <u>thing</u> I had wanted--a toy to stimulate my imagination, not a musical instrument. My father was smart. I had what I wanted, and all it cost him was a few hours of his time.

TELEVISION

For Christmas in 1949, when I was in the third grade, my classmate Robert Wells' family got a television set, the first in town as far as I knew. His father, a pharmacist, owned Wells' Drug Store, so by Mount Vernon standards he was rich.

The first time I saw television was probably shortly after that. On the way home from a shopping trip to Seattle we stopped for dinner somewhere north of the city. As we were shown to our table we passed the counter, behind which was a table model TV set with a screen about six inches wide. The program was "The Lone Ranger." I recognized the theme song, "William Tell Overture," from the radio program. Sure enough, there were the masked man, his faithful Indian companion, Tonto, and his great horse SILVER galloping across the screen. I was hooked.

My father, however, was not. Gradually, houses in the neighborhood displayed the new status symbol, the antenna on the roof, indicating a TV set in the living room. First were the Cannons, across the street; I was invited to watch a few times in their darkened living room. At this point there was only one Seattle station, channel 5, and it only broadcast programs certain hours of the day. At other times it broadcast a test pattern--a circle in a square with identical designs in each corner, whose purpose was to enable the viewer to adjust the picture using the knobs for horizontal and vertical hold. Then the Farrell family down the alley got TV. Their kids were much younger than I, but once their oldest, Patrick, invited me to watch "Howdy Doody." By then I was in fourth grade and thought the program was silly, but I was thrilled to see it just the same.

After Sharon's family moved to Bellevue, they got TV. When I went to visit, we all sat in the dark in the evening and watched. They were so close to Seattle that they didn't need an antenna on the roof--just rabbit ears attached to the TV. A new product was the TV lamp, a dim light which sat on top of the TV and was supposed to help avoid eye strain caused by watching TV in a dark room. In sixth grade half the kids in Mr. Clark's room had TV and talked about a popular program, "I Love Lucy." When the Merryweathers next door got TV they invited me over to watch "I Love Lucy" every week, so I was able to participate in the discussion at school the next day. Connie Cook's family got a 21-inch console with "halo light," which was supposed to serve the purpose of the TV lamp. Daddy was still not persuaded, though I hit him with every argument in my arsenal including, "I need it for my education."

By seventh grade Auntie Ruth and Uncle Del had TV, with an antenna stuck in the ground in their yard. This made it easy to turn the antenna as needed to get the best reception. Florence and Harry Seline, friends of my parents who lived east of Sedro Woolley and had no indoor toilet, just an outhouse, got TV. The reception was so bad that it was mostly "snow," but they insisted we watch it as a treat when visiting.

In the summer after seventh grade, when Patricia's family moved to the farm, they got TV. Her father worked at Sears and got a good deal on a floor-model TV with a bonus: a bottom drawer which pulled out to reveal a 3-speed record player. It seemed that my family and Annaly's were the only ones still deprived. Then, at the beginning of eighth grade, even Annaly got TV.

Since everyone around me had TV I had ample opportunity to watch. "Wild Bill Hickok," starring my hero Guy Madison, was on with a new episode once a week and re-runs two more times a week. I rotated among the Merryweathers', Auntie Ruth's and Annaly's to catch three shows a week, getting my "Guy" fix. On Saturdays it became routine that right after dinner I went to Annaly's for evening TV. Her parents sat in their easy chairs at one end of the living room, the TV sat at the opposite end, and Annaly and I occupied the couch along one wall. First we watched "Beat the Clock"; then "The Jackie Gleason Show" with the June Taylor Dancers and the battling "Honeymooners"; "The George Gobel Show" with pretty, perky Peggy King, a singer; and finally, "Your Hit Parade" featuring Giselle MacKenzie, Dorothy Collins, Snooky Lanson, and Russell Arms, who sang and dramatized the week's top ten popular songs. For Instance, Giselle sang "Let Me Go, Lover" while trapped in a big rope spider web, with one of the male singers as a spider in coat and tails. When a song stayed on top for many weeks, as did "The Ballad of Davy Crockett" ("...born on a mountain top in

Tennessee...") the producers' creativity was sorely challenged. Somewhere during this time Lawrence Welk's program debuted, and Annaly's parents were among his fans. Annaly and I delighted in making fun of Lawrence and his performers, especially the sad-sack violinist and the "Lovely Lennon Sisters," whom we called the Lovely Lemon Sisters.

One fall afternoon when Annaly and I walked home from our first year of high school, we spotted a "Hugo Helmer" panel truck parked in front of our house. Helmer's store sold sheet music, musical instruments, and, for some reason, television sets. We stopped in our tracks. "Janet," said Annaly, "do you think--?" We speeded up and soon saw an antenna attached to our chimney. I couldn't believe it!

Daddy said he was just trying it out to see how good the reception was, but I knew the battle was won. Though I was too old for that new show for kids, "The Mickey Mouse Club," I watched it anyway every day after school. Someone gave us a TV lamp for Christmas. Soon, though, my interest in TV waned as I became involved in high school activities. One Saturday night when I answered the phone Uncle Del said, "Tell your Dad to turn on channel 4."

"Oh no!" I said.

"Oh yes," said Del, "champagne music!" He had discovered Lawrence Welk. Every Saturday night for the rest of his life Daddy watched Lawrence Welk. He enjoyed having TV much more than I ever did.

CLOSURE

SWEEPING UP
July 1983

In three days I empty the house my parents built over fifty years ago. At the end there is no time for thoughtful sorting through pictures, for choosing keepsakes, for recalling the once white crispness of a limp, gray grosgrain ribbon found among the paint cans and dust in the garage. Memories flare briefly and subside, quenched by expediency.

White grosgrain ribbon--freshly ironed red, pink, blue, plaid, they hung by the kitchen door where now I remove a can opener from the wall. I will take it for my mother to use at my house, where she will live now. Every morning, from 8:30 to 8:45, I sat on my little red chair (what became of it, and when?) while my mother combed and braided my hair. I held a glass of water (which once contained cheese spread) in which she dipped the comb. I cringed as drops fell on my shoulders, whimpering as she yanked snarls, racing the clock. Ribbons provided a finishing touch. When I was nine she gave in to my campaign for short hair. After my father took the photo she cut off the braids, using rubber bands to secure the raw ends, arranged them in a flat box, and carefully placed it in her cedar chest. Last week, before the movers came, she and I discovered it.

She told me then, again, how my father had made the cedar chest and brought it to her in his Model-T at Christmas, before they were married. When her family gather round to admire, someone set her niece, Barbara, inside. As the story goes, Barbara soaked her diaper, Christening the cedar chest.

Barbara, her daughter Beth, Beth's husband, Aunt Ruth (my only living aunt), and neighbors--an army of helpers--sort, sweep, discard, salvage, clean. A dumpster, delivered by the city's sanitation department, occupies the driveway. We fill it twice, and Beth drives her loaded pickup to the dump four times. Beth wants the organ my father made. They haul it down from the attic but cannot maneuver it through the stair door and have to take it back up. How did my father get it upstairs? Or did he build it there? We leave it for the new people.

Several pairs of overalls, which he once used in his floor sanding business and later kept for working on the car, remain hanging in the garage. Iin later years his work clothes were tan or gray shirts and pants from J.C. Penney. A neighbor tosses the overalls in the dumpster while I am occupied elsewhere.

Trash from the basement they throw out the window, and from there into the pickup. Dozens of carefully hoarded amber glass jars and jugs, holding chemicals for developing pictures, some gathering dust for forty years, go without ceremony. A tall wooden stool--the one I sat on while my father developed pictures--is kicked aside to make room for moving a cast iron printing press up the stairs.

My mother used the printing press (found in an Anacortes warehouse) for linoleum block printing, to earn extra money. She blocked pre-cut pieces of fabric which she mailed to California. There, her cousin Winifred sewed them into smocks for an organization called Allied Artists. The rollers and ink had to be ordered from California, and my father carved the blocks from battleship linoleum, heated over a hot plate which came with the popcorn popper. Some days my mother spent all afternoon in the basement "blocking." One day, when I came home from school in the eighth grade, Grandma told me to go downstairs, that my mother had something to tell me. Mom's eyes said it was bad, and she began to cry. "Mickey died." I fled. Mickey, my bright green parakeet, who chirped "Pretty Mickey" to his reflection in the bathroom mirror, lay stiff in the bottom of his cage in the dining room. I carried him to my room and wept, gently stroking his feathers. We buried him under the forsythia by the clothesline pole.

I reclaim the wrought iron birdcage stand from the basement, where it has been almost as long as the old Philco radio. I will paint the stand black and use it as a hanging plant stand. A Boston fern will look nice.

On my stomach, in front of the Philco, I listened to my favorite children's radio programs. One time I sent in a quarter and a label from Quaker Puffed Rice, which I had to eat until the box was empty, to get a special ring described before, during, and after "Tom Mix." Eagerly, the announcer declared that, mounted on the ring ("made to fit any finger") was a tiny six-shooter which shot--"listen to this, kids, REAL SPARKS!" Just what I needed to fend off the boogeyman Grandma worried about. Weeks later it arrived. Hardly the flames I had envisioned, the sparks came from a tiny flint which wore out that same day. Within a week, the gun broke off. What remained of the ring, my mother placed on a shelf above the kitchen sink. It got pushed aside, first by cactus plants, later by African violets. Now some African violets have been removed to my house in Tacoma, where my mother waits for me. The ring has been saved long enough.

The antique dealer arrives in her van to make a killing. I know her game but lack time and interest to play it. As she leaves she tells me my storybook dolls are worth the most of what she takes, but too bad I hadn't saved the polka dot boxes. I have saved just one of the dolls--my first.

Next come the used furniture people, who take several pieces including my bed, bought as part of my high school home economics decorating project. A neighbor fills her station wagon twice with jetsam for a garage sale. Others come to sift through the leavings, which I sell or give away. We focus on the main floor, closing off rooms as we finish with them, until only the living room and kitchen remain.

A voice at General Telephone's central business office has told me how to disconnect and remove the wall phone so I can return it to them. Someone is talking on the party line as I clip the wires, abruptly stopping the tinny staccato. I toss the phone in my car and scribble "turn in phone" on my to-do list.

The Salvation Army truck pulls up. I help load the clothing and boxes heaped in the living room. When the truck drives off, nothing remains but a few scraps. Forty-five minutes later I have finished vacuuming and sweep the last of the trash through the kitchen, out the door and into the dumpster.

Alone, I linger. Tomorrow a new family will "take possession." I walk through each room for the last time, reflecting on the secrets within these walls: that the small hole in the ceiling of the downstairs bedroom (the room where, most likely, I was conceived and where I slept for the first seven years of my life) was drilled thirty years ago so a string could pass to my parents' room above. Grandma, needing to relieve herself in the night, would pull the string to ring a bell and awaken my mother. I hated that bell in the night, disturbing my mother's sleep--though I loved Grandma. Another secret: that a knot hole, three inches across, lies in a wide board beneath the hardwood floor in my upstairs bedroom. Secret: that behind the plaster of the living room wall, above where the TV stood until last week, is a stovepipe opening. Before the oil furnace, before the coal furnace, before me, a wood stove heated that part of the house. Secret: that in the early morning little more than two years ago my father died, here on the living room floor, surrounded by paramedics, stretched out between the piano and the TV. Secret: that in the ground by the old clothesline pole behind the garage rest the bones of a parakeet.

Now I feel as I did when I viewed my father's body in the funeral home. I know that it is my last look, and I hope for a sense of finality: it is over; time to leave. Goodbye. Spoken aloud, the word echoes through the rooms, but the feeling eludes me. Soon--because further delay seems foolish and I am hungry--I take the key I have carried for thirty years and add it to the collection on the kitchen table. "Keys to house and garage," reads my note. The front door locks automatically behind me. I walk to Aunt Ruth's house for a shower and supper before the long drive home. My mother will live with me for almost five years, and in a nearby nursing home for another three before dying a few days after her ninety-third birthday.

MY PARENTS

My parents were and still are so much of who I am, and are so much a part of this narrative, that perhaps I need not devote a special section to them. Nevertheless, some comments about them will perhaps make a fitting conclusion. I often wished that they had had two children, not just so I would have had a sibling, but also because maybe that child and my mother could have been what my father and I were to each other: two peas in a pod. We spent many golden hours together. I was definitely my Daddy's girl, definitely a Grimes, not a Ward. Mom once said the only thing about me that was like her was the color of my eyes. Daddy and I were on the same wave length, whereas I simply didn't understand her. Lots of things about her annoyed me--her goofiness over her dogs, for example, or her refusal to discuss things that bothered her, or her black and white provincial "Mount Vernon" view of the world. We seemed to disagree on everything trivial. More than once I drove her to tears, which of course made me feel terrible too.

On the other hand, my father drove me to tears. We disagreed on what seemed to me the big things, such as when I was ready to get my driver's license or whether I could go to college away from home. We thought so much alike, laughed at the same things, were interested in so many of the same things, that I always expected him to see things my way. On visits home from college I hoped to share with him my intellectual awakening. But some of the literature (William Faulkner) I brought home upset him. When he said, after a heated discussion, "I've lost you, somehow," I broke into tears, knowing that he hadn't lost me at all, that because of him I was hungry for the liberal education I was getting. When I broke down, it was my mother who put her arms around me. She just wanted me to be happy; she didn't care what I thought.

With her own money my mother had bought me dancing lessons, piano lessons, and a piano, all of which I took as my right but would not have had except for her. Shortly before she died, someone who knew us both said, "You are your mother's daughter." He was referring to our stubbornness, but by then I knew that we were more alike than I had realized. We both were naturally very shy. She enjoyed people she knew, but she was not good at getting to know them. I understood that perfectly, because I felt the same and had to force myself to make the first move. As a young child I clung to my mother when among strangers. I refused to sit at the children's table with some of my older cousins and distant relatives at Big Lake, even though a boy who could barely walk was the opposite, refusing to sit beside his mother at the adult table. He wanted to be with the other kids.

In contrast to all of our everyday bickering, I remember one golden afternoon when my mother and I were in perfect harmony. I was eleven or twelve, and we went fishing, an activity that normally caused a whiney objection to swell in the back of my throat. Perhaps my father told me I had to go with her, that she needed this break and that my going with her was important. For whatever reason, I went without protest to one of those numbered lakes (Lake Ten or Lake Sixteen) east of town where we climbed down a steep bank to the lake and climbed aboard the raft floating there in dappled sunlight. With poles or paddles, we moved out into the small lake and let the raft drift. I don't remember if Mom caught any fish, or if we had our lunch with us, though probably we did. What I do remember was how pleasant and peaceful it was, the two of us at one with each other and with nature.

The older I grow the more I appreciate what it took for my parents to raise me. My mother was almost forty-two when I was born; my father was thirty-nine. They had been married eleven years, had lived through the Great Depression which wasn't over yet, and during that time it was my mother who had the steady job. My father told me that she cried when she learned she was pregnant. Grandma said, "Why Hazel, I'm tickled to death!" and years later Mom told me Aunt Claire had asked, "What are you going to do about it?" and that her answer was, "Nothing." I said, "Well, what could you have done about it?" "I could have had an abortion," she replied. I was so shocked I didn't think to ask how such illegal things were done in those days. Maybe the women she worked with at the telephone office had their ways.

So I was born and proved to be even more a disruption than anticipated, with colic for three months straight and intermittently for three more. Mom always shuddered when recalling those first months of my life. How fortunate my parents and I were to have a family support network close by at that time. She had quit her job, because Daddy felt a mother should stay at home with her child--something I took for granted as I grew up and now realize what a rich childhood I had because of it. Daddy's floor sanding business began to pick up, and then the War happened, the economy boomed, and we all survived. My world expanded, and I proceeded to become who I am.

Our last picture together--May 1981

WHO'S WHO

Alice and Charlie Kennedy--Mom's cousin and husband; Aunt Belle's daughter
Annaly McPherson--classmate and neighborhood friend
Aunt Belle--Grandma's sister, my great-aunt
Aunt Carol Egan--Dad's sister
Aunt Claire Maris--Mom's sister
Aunt Maggie--Grandma's sister, my great-aunt
Aunt Mary (Mamie)--Grandma's sister, my great-aunt
Aunt Ruth Van Sickle--Dad's sister
Aunt Siddie--Grandma's sister, my great-aunt
Barbara Breathour--my cousin, Mom & Aunt Claire's niece
Bob Egan--my cousin; Dad's nephew
B. family--neighbors down the alley (playmates Bobby and Mark)
Butch-cat--the cat of my childhood
Butch-dog--Grandpa's dog
Cannon (Mr. & Mrs.)--elderly neighbors across the street; Lonnie's grandparents
Curtis Graybeal--Barbara's second husband
Dad--Forrest Grimes, my father
Danny--cousin Barbara's son
Elly Rouw--classmate and neighborhood playmate
Grandma--Annie (Knox) Ward, maternal grandmother
Grandpa--James Grimes, paternal grandfather
Grandpa Britt--Roggie's stepfather
Jimmy Jacobs--Uncle Ed & Nina's son; my Dad's cousin
Joey Kenna--pre-school neighborhood playmate
Kathy Lindquist--classmate and neighborhood playmate
Kay Van Sickle--my cousin; Dad's niece
Larry Van Sickle--my cousin; Dad's nephew
Lonnie Varnadore--pre-school playmate; Cannon's grandson
Marge/Margie Egan--my cousin; Dad's niece
McClusky family--neighbors down the alley (playmates Billy and Bobby)
Merryweather family (Esther, Dick, Gloria, Ann)--next-door neighbors
Mrs. Flinnigan--my imaginary, sophisticated, grown-up persona
Mom--Hazel (Ward) Grimes, my mother
Nancy Wynstra--classmate and neighborhood playmate
Nina Jacobs--Uncle Ed's wife
Patricia Davis--classmate and best friend from 7th grade through high school

Ray Bloom--classmate & neighborhood friend
Rusty--the dog of my childhood
Schacht (Mr. & Mrs.)--elderly neighbors across the alley (after Watsons moved)
Sharon Peterson--classmate and neighborhood friend; best grade school friend
Snooky--Kay's cat
Timmy (Timothy McGillicuddy)--Aunt Claire's dog
Uncle Del Van Sickle--Aunt Ruth's husband
Uncle Ed Jacobs--Dad's uncle
Uncle Howard Egan--Aunt Carol's husband
Uncle Roggie (Ralph Maris)--Aunt Claire's husband
Watson family--neighbors across the alley; later moved
Will Knox--Grandma's only brother
Winifred--Great-aunt Mary's daughter; Mom's cousin

ABOUT THE AUTHOR

Janet Grimes was born in Mount Vernon, Washington November 8, 1940 and couldn't wait to get out of there. At age eighteen she finally did by going to college one hundred miles to the south in Tacoma. After graduation, four years in the Midwest and one trip to Europe, she realized Western Washington was a great place to live and returned to Tacoma and a job teaching at Tacoma Community College. Retired since 1996, she has traveled extensively in the United States and Europe but is happy to return to Tacoma where she lives with her husband Bob and two cats. She returns to Mount Vernon frequently to visit with friends and relatives and to check up on her old haunts.

Made in United States
Troutdale, OR
12/21/2025

44448448R10100